Log On!

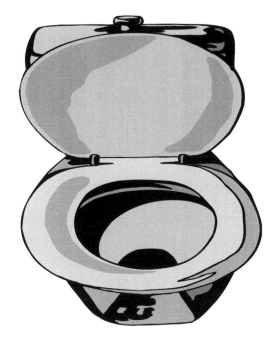

The Big Book of Bowel Movements

Written by
Kelly P. Gray

Author's Note

My objective in writing this book, is to make you laugh. I have had the idea for this book in my head now for over five years. I cannot explain my fascination with bowel movements, but I can say that I enjoy them immensely, and I think there are many of you readers who do also. This book is for you, those who revel in an outstanding dump and love to tell people about it.

There are those people who feel that the bowel movement is a topic never to be spoken of; but what or who are we hiding from? Let's get it out in the open, we all do it, some with more or less success than others, but who cares? I doubt very much if there isn't a person reading this book that can't tell a great bowel movement story. This book is meant to be set on your coffee table and laughed at openly between friends, neighbors and family. Then again, if you choose to keep it in the bathroom, I would also consider that an honor. I hope this book helps bring us all together in an increasingly crazy and turbulent world. A little laughter never hurt anyone, especially when you're talking about a huge, messy dump that slipped down your shorts in a grocery store.

The years have passed since I first thought of the idea for this book, but my interest in this taboo topic has not waned, it has in fact, greatened. I have put together a few chapters on the intricacies I find interesting, regarding the bowel movement. You will be surprised at how many details and thoughts I have gathered relating to taking a dump. I have a small group of warped friends and family who enjoy sharing bowel movement stories with each other. This isn't a macho thing, we don't always talk about how huge our dump was or how bad it smelled, but in fact, many of our tales come from our most embarrassing moments. I have left a few pages at the end for your notes, I encourage you to write down your thoughts and ideas and send me an e-mail or visit www.thebigbookofbowelmovements.com I hope you find this book entertaining and hopefully, you'll be able to share your favorite moment with a friend or loved one.

Kelly P. Gray

Dedication

I dedicate this book to a select few individuals who have inspired me from the past to the present.

My dad, Larry, God rest his soul; who called going poop, "Going Big". My mother, Pat, who suffered from Irritable bowel Syndrome, so you can imagine the stories she told. Mark Sorenson, my amigo and co-founder of the World Bowel Movement Association. Counselor Jake Stub, my insane friend with some great dumps. My brother, Mike, who has begun pushing me to do a "Dump Magazine", complete with a dump of the month fold out. My oldest brother Gary, who has single handedly set the world record for consistently producing the worst skid marks ever. My friend Bob Howe, who revels in his daily movements, and who loves to tell a good "dump in the pants" story. My dogs, past and present are a daily inspiration, here's to you, Shiner, Hana, Dobie, Paki, Chrissy, Bailey, Rainy and Puka. Our cat Wednesday has also taken up a strange new habit, she is taking her dumps in the yard like a dog. Amber, our daughter, who wrote the book on constipation, and her oldest daughter, Attle. The last and most important person in my life is my wife Elaine. She is still a "closet pooper"; the door still

has to be closed, but is starting to open up. I love you.

Table Of Contents

Chapter One

Foods and The Curious Dumps They Produce

We all know food plays an important role in the kind of dump we produce. The food we partake in, can make or break us the next morning. When you really think about it, the food and drink we consume controls the color, size, texture and aroma of our daily bowel movements.. We are in complete control of our daily dump destiny.

Just like many facets of our life, we do things that feel good at the time, but pay for, at a later date. Dumps are not any different. We can't fool our bowels, If we eat it or drink it, we'll see it later, in some form. Sometimes I'll have a night in which I get caught up in drinking and forget to eat, and in that case, I might throw up and throw caution to the wind, as far as the next day's dump goes.

We all go through times of consistent and inconsistent bowel movements. I, for one, pride myself on a daily, morning dump between 7:00 a.m. and 9:00 a.m. I'll be honest, any alteration from my schedule, puts me on edge throughout the day, until I finally take a dump. I have come to realize that my diet is the main cog in the wheel of dumping.

Let's get this out in the open right now, all of us at one time or another have stepped up from the toilet, turned around and admired our work. It is a fact of life, the human is a curious animal.; and when a curious, but exciting object comes out of our butt with an extraordinary size, shape, consistency or smell, we have to look at it. I get a reassuring and comfortable feeling when I look down into the toilet to admire my work, knowing it was my creation, a part of me. I am not a woman, but I think this is the closest a man gets to giving birth. I received a call from my mother, Pat a few weeks ago, and she told me she had to call to tell me that she had just taken a "four foot long rope". Now that is admiration in it's finest hour. I wonder how many of you are going through life producing these works of art, these little joy gems that we leave behind and flush down the toilet, never to spoken of, or shared with again. Turn to the "Turn around and admire your work" chapter, for more discussion on this topic.

We have all seen or heard the effects that peanuts and corn have on our bowel movements. It really is a marvel of science that a whole piece of food can pass through our complicated systems, without a scratch. The corn and the peanut don't play by the same rules as the other foods, and they know it. The corn kernel probably races by the sloth- like squash, and thumbs his nose at him. The cocky peanut just laughs at the slow moving sirloin. The corn and the peanut are "wise guys", you know, the type that gets away with murder. They have it easy, they don't even have to hang out in the dirty part of town, they just race by in their new, shiny cars. Remember this when you pop a peanut into your mouth or nibble off an ear of corn; give them each a little extra chew, they deserve it. I have wondered if this principle applies to a peanut with the shell on. Ouch! Now don't get me wrong, the corn is not all bad.

You have to admit it, corn adds a little levity to the toilet bowl. I like corn and in fact, it is my favorite vegetable, and maybe because I like it when they add some color to my dumps. In a world of brown hues, the corn kernel brightens up the dump. It makes me happy when I whirl around and admire my dump, and I see these little happy circles of yellow swimming around. Corn in the dump is like the circus when it comes to town. Picture a small, lifeless, plain town stuck somewhere in the Midwest, always the same people doing the same inane things, until, word comes that the circus is coming to town! This changes the whole scene, from drab and lifeless, to colorful and fun. I feel this way when corn comes to visit my dreary toilet bowl. I remember my mom making us something called Goulash, when we were kids. When I think about it, that goulash looked a lot like one of my dumps with corn in it. Corn also has an ally, butter. I don't think I ever eat corn whether it is fresh, frozen or in corn bread, that I don't slather on a ton of butter. May be that is the reason for the corn slipping by so easily down there. I'll have to conduct some serious research.

There has been a debate in my household ever since I married Elaine. The debate rages over cheese, and how it affects the dump. Elaine claims that cheese stops her up, and I swear that is loosens up everything and slides on through. The topic will inevitably come up every time we're out eating pizza. I'll order extra cheese and she'll say, "that should stop me up for a few days," and I'll always argue the opposite. We'll continue bantering back and forth until she finally changes the subject. She may claim stoppage with cheese, but I have proof to the contrary. I have seen her eat some Jalapeno Jack cheese on one day, and be shooting flames out her butt the next. There is my proof, and the jalapenos had nothing to do with it. Our thirty five year old daughter; and for sake of not totally humiliating her, I'll refer to her by "Amber"; lays claim to her mothers cheese

theory. She says that cheese stops her up for days on end, and I believe her. I
have seen Amber go seven and even eight days without taking a bowel
movement! I would have committed suicide, I'm so paranoid about my dumps,
that if I leave the house in the morning without going, I'll worry about it all day
until it happens. See the Constipation chapter for more on this pleasant subject.

Let's discuss lettuce. What is the deal with lettuce? I can eat a nice Caesar
salad, complete with Romaine lettuce, cheese, croutons and dressing, and an hour
later, I'll have to take dump and there it is. The Romaine lettuce is floating on top
of the toilet water enjoying a swim. It always looks like I didn't even chew it,
there are whole pieces of lettuce floating around in my toilet. I might as well save
some money, fish it out, rinse it off and toss another salad, I can't believe it. Now
don't get the wrong idea, this type of activity doesn't bother me, in fact I am quite
appreciative of it's resourcefulness, but I still can't explain why this happens. The
romaine lettuce must be like those guys you see, while you're waiting in line to
get into a club. You know the type, they casually walk up to the doorman, slip
him something, and wham, he's in the door! I don't like those types of people

and I'm sure that romaine, corn and peanuts are those types down in the bowel society.

I could go on forever listing all the types of foods and their curious dump counterparts, but I'll stick to a few I find fascinating. Let's discuss the world of hot dogs. I love hot dogs, all kinds of them, from the most mild mannered Oscar Mayer through the German Bratwursts to the gnarliest of Italian sausages. I'll be honest with you, I pay for my actions when I consume these babies. I have heard all the stories about what goes into the making of a hot dog, but I really don't care. I cover my dog with mustard, relish, onions and kraut, if it's handy. The hot dog dump is a good dump. It is usually a solid, compact dump with a small to moderate amount of wiping and a thick smell. My current favorite hot dog is a spicy Italian sausage sold by a vendor by the stadium here in Seattle. It is spicy and stuffed with cheese but my anus will pay for it on Monday mornings. It sometimes feels like my ass is on flames. It feels like I could bend over and shoot flames out my butt. I have to double check my toilet paper after wiping, just to make sure there isn't any blood. I always peruse the hot dog section of the supermarket , to make sure there isn't another type that has come into the marketplace I haven't tried. The Kosher style dog is outstanding! Huge dump the next morning with little or no smell. I have another interesting question, is pepperoni considered a hot dog? If it is, I have to give it a ten on hot dog dump gnarly scale. I try to make it to Costco once in awhile to have their hot dog and a soda for $1.62. If I ever get in financial dire straights, I know I could exist on $3.24 a day because at Costco, you get a huge Polish sausage and an unlimited soda for $1.62. When I feel like a big spender, I take Elaine out to lunch there. My point here is that this dog produces a great dump, never fail. Elaine and I have taken a few trips to Europe and had the pleasure to sample Germany's Bratwursts. Elaine ate a few, but I had to stop at least once a day to pound down a Brat. On our first trip, I completely blew her out of our hotel rooms on a nightly basis. They were gnarly, but satisfying dumps but the odor factor was huge. Elaine was constipated for eleven days on that trip! The Bratwursts must have stopped her up, but more on that story a little later. My point here is the hot dog in any shape, size or color, produces a fine bowel movement.

I am a toast guy. I eat toast almost every day of my life and I happen to believe that toast is a major contributor to my dumping success. Have you ever watched your mother or wife put together a meat loaf? They always put in bread or soda crackers. The only purpose they serve is to keep the loaf together; to keep it from falling apart. A bowel movement is nothing more than a smelly meat loaf. Maybe this is where the expression, "Pinch a loaf", came from. This theory can be applied to my dumps, I consistently produce a firm, solid dump on a daily basis and I attribute this to my toast intake. Go for the toast if you're having loose or inconsistent stools.

Cereal is a great dump producer. I don't eat much cereal, but I do feel it has it's good qualities pertaining to the bowel movement. I do love a bowl of Captain Crunch once in awhile and with a piece of toast alongside, I will always produce a stellar dump. I don't believe in those Bran types of cereals. I am a purist and I don't believe in artificially enhanced dumps. Coffee and Bran falls into this category. They are both anal stimulators and they are wrong to use if you're trying to stimulate your sphincter. It's like the East Germans using those steroids during the Olympics; you remember, the women all looked like Arnold Schwarzenegger. I don' believe in artificial stimulation when it comes to taking a good, old fashioned dump. Submarine sandwiches are great dump producers.

They sometimes surprise me with how fast they whiz their way through my system. I mentioned earlier that I am a one dump a day guy, but I'll make exception to that rule with a good foot long Sub. I find that when I consume one of these babies for lunch, I sometimes find myself summoned to the bathroom in the evening or in the middle of the night. I know it is the foot long causing the night dump, but it disturbs me for one reason. I always fear for the quality of the next day's dump. Whenever I have to take a dump in the evening, I worry my dump will suffer the next morning or even be non existent. This is a tough decision for me, because I can go in the evening and hope for the best the next morning, basically mortgage my morning dump; or I can hold the mouse in, (See chapter 3), and hope for a monster dump the next morning. Life is full of tough decisions.

I think the mayonnaise has a lubricating effect on the sandwich. "It lubricates as it protects." It is truly an art to make a great sandwich. My dad, Larry always wanted to open a deli, but I think he would have eaten the profits, but he always, every time put together the greatest sandwiches. He always used mayo, and he wasn't shy about it, but not too much as to ruin the flavor the meat. He always used mustard, and loved to work with tomatoes and onions. I notice an oil and vinegar option at most sandwich shops nowadays, and I go for it, I think it helps in making sure the package slides down through your system without any problems.

Elaine loves hot peppers. She would put them in her cereal if I let her. She puts them on almost everything. You should see her and Bob together when he comes over for dinner. They are like wild animals foraging through the fridge, looking for jalapenos or some other type of hot pepper to put in their food. I can't grill them a hamburger anymore, without first mixing hot peppers in their hamburger meat. Elaine bakes cornbread with jalapenos mixed into the batter, but has to leave me a small sliver of cornbread without jalapenos. She also loves those crushed up red and yellow peppers you see at pizza places. I try those on my pizza and I can't feel my tongue for an hour. Yes, she loves those peppers, but she pays for it on the toilet. She'll walk out of our bathroom after taking a pepper dump, and have this weird look on her face. I immediately start laughing when she tells me that she has a "burny butt".

Ethnic foods produce some great, but gnarly dumps. I have to admit, I don't eat much of the spicy stuff, but I partake once in awhile when I'm feeling brave. I love hot and sour soup at our local Chinese restaurant. Wow, talk about flames shooting out of your butt, I have to put on asbestos gloves, just to wipe myself the next morning. I also love to order Kung Pao chicken, with those little, nasty red peppers sprinkled throughout. If I bite into one of those babies, I'm definitely good for another beer or two. I actually think this red pepper is the same as the pepper in the pizza sprinkles. This produces the kind of dump that I even hate to smell. You know you have taken the wrong eating path, when you can't stand the smell of your own bowel movement. The smell of your own dump should always be a pleasant experience. I love Mexican food and I eat it probably once a week, if not more. Sure , we all know about beans, being good for your heart and all, but I always seem to have a pretty normal and satisfying dump after my Mexican meal. I will add a recent guacamole experience, however. I ordered and ate some Taquitos smothered in guacamole, and I love the stuff, but my poop the next morning was like a huge, brown pile of stinky guacamole. It looked like a huge pile of wet sand or freshly mixed concrete, sitting there at the bottom of the toilet bowl. It was a three or four wipe experience.

My wife thinks I'm crazy, but I have been keeping these little notepads stationed at all my toilets around the house for years. My latest entry raises a curious question. Why is poop always brown? We eat red peppers, yellow squash, green beans, oranges, purple grapes, blueberries and blackberries, but our poop always comes out brown. Do we have a little ink jet in our sphincters that only uses the brown ink cartridge? Maybe the ink jet is clogged, I could definitely see this happening. Now, I have found an exception to this rule. For you drinkers out there, and I'm one of you; there is a liqueur named Opal Nera. It is a licorice flavored liqueur, (actually, to be technical, the licorice flavor is derived from anise, pronounced an-is). I suppose if it was pronounced like "anus", it would open a whole new can of worms for the bar business. You'd have regulars ordering another round of "anus juice", or you'd hear a cocktail girl hollering for another round of "butt cracks" on the rocks. They would be able to invent many catchy drink names, like the hairy butt, the butt crack, or how about a spin on a popular brunch cocktail, the bloody butt! Anyway, Opal Nera is licorice tasting, but the liqueur is pure black. The odd connection between this drink and your bowel movement, is that your poop comes out bright green! No joke here, this is serious stuff, bright green! Try it sometime, it will amaze friends and family alike.

I would need to create a treatise, in order to cover all the foods and drinks that help in creating odd or wonderful bowel movements, but I think you get my point. This subject will inevitably come up in more detail in the second installment of "Big Book." The dumps we produce are a direct reflection of the food we consume. I am aware that there are now urine tests being conducted by companies in order to insure a potential clean employee. I'm just glad to know there aren't any bowel movement tests, I'd fail miserably. The next time you sit down and produce a dump of enviable quality or one of disastrous proportions, think back on what you ate, it might help you next time to either reverse the trend or create another masterpiece.

Chapter Two

Constipation

To tell you the truth, I don't like this subject, I don't like it all. My wife felt that I needed to touch on the subject for those of you who do experience this malady; the heartbreak of constipation. I live with this problem; not personally, but with my wife, daughter and my dogs on rare occasion.

I didn't want to write about this horrible topic, but Elaine has urged me to include a few thoughts and stories that might help ease the pain for those of you who suffer from constipation. I am not perfect, I have had a few bouts of constipation, but I can count them on one hand. I actually went to the emergency ward of a local hospital one night because I was stopped up. Do you think I over reacted just a bit? Well, just like I said, I take my bowel movements very seriously. I had just had a minor surgery to my ankle and I was on pain pills. Pain pills are a definite poop inhibitor. I don't think I had taken a dump in two days and I was stressing over it. I was a good dad and made homemade macaroni for Elaine and Amber. Just after we had finished, I felt this horrible pain in my stomach. I went into the bedroom, climbed on the bed and started rolling around, trying to get rid of the pain. It felt like my insides were about to burst. At first I thought it was the macaroni, but Elaine then asked me how long it had been since I had taken a dump. It suddenly hit me, I was constipated. I rolled back on forth on the bed like a little baby and I tried to withstand the pain. It felt like I had fifteen pounds of poop stuck inside of me, you see, I was a newcomer to the world of constipation. The pain was excruciating as I crawled to the toilet. I sat up and tried to let it loose, but no dice. I was corked up like a wine bottle. Elaine wouldn't watch any longer, she put a jacket on me and drove me to the hospital. I didn't know if my appendix were bursting or if I had swallowed rat poison, but I did know that it was hurting bad. Elaine pulls up to the emergency ward door and I'm nearly in tears. Who ever heard of going to the hospital for constipation! I don't remember what happened next, but all of a sudden while I'm sitting there waiting for a doctor, I jumped up from my chair and ran into the bathroom. Elaine must have covered her face, with the way I was acting. It felt like Mount Vesuvius was ready to blow it's top, and in a weird way, it was kind of exciting, but scary too. Now, I am not the type of person who embarrasses easily, but that night was an exception. I barely got my sweats down around my ankles, when the volcano blew.

The walls came crumbling down, the building shook and I could hear the scream of the people in the waiting room as they scrambled for cover. I nearly bumped my head on the ceiling as the blast propelled me into the air as I let loose the most amazing buildup of poop and gas you can imagine. The sound reverberated off the walls and thundered out into the waiting room. If I had this on tape, I'd be famous. I felt like my stomach was a full balloon that had let out all it's air. I must say that the looks I received from the other patients as I emerged from that bathroom were incredulous. I was embarrassed to the hilt, but some where back in my warped little mind, I also felt a strange feeling of pride. Elaine shook her head at me as I approached her. It was a performance for the ages, and in public too! Elaine didn't say a word as she led me out of the waiting room. She was about five steps ahead of me, pretending not to know me. We drove home in silence, but I had a big, shit eating grin on my face.

Constipation comes in a few different forms. Constipation is when you are stopped up sure, but there are other forms. You know those bowel movements when you sit down and then grunt, groan and struggle red faced to only produce a little Mild Dud like, pooplet. You are kidding yourself if you get satisfaction from a turd the size of a marble. Pooplets, marbles, and Milk Duds count as constipation. I mentioned earlier that I can set my watch each morning by my bowel movement. I don't take it for granted, and in fact, I am a little scared my good fortunes will change when I get older, but I think if I do suffer from an old age dumping dilemma, it will be the opposite of constipation. My biggest dilemma will be how many pairs of Depends to pack before going on vacation. I have brought up the topic of adult underpants to my Seahawk, season ticket holding friend, Bob. I don't like waiting in those huge lines to take a pee, so I thought about wearing Depends, so I won't miss any of the action. He won't go for it. My point here is don't let constipation creep up on you, it comes in many forms.

I married Elaine in April of 1988, and she is a wonderful woman, but she has a warped perspective on bowel movements. She has gone her entire life with the idea that if she takes a dump every four or five days, that it's okay! Wow! No way, no how, for this kid here. I'd be jumping off the Space Needle if I went that long without taking a dump. She goes through life happy as a clam to take one or two dumps a week. This is crazy, I know, but I live with it.

Elaine and I took a trip to Europe back in 1990, spending three weeks exploring the countryside's of Germany, Austria and Switzerland. We rented a car and stayed in Hotels or Hostels, so we had access to bathrooms all along the way. I found the food and drink of Bavaria, much to my liking. I had to stop every three or four towns for a Bratwurst and a cold stein of German beer. Much to my pleasure, Elaine was enjoying the cuisine as much as I. I was also enjoying unprecedented success in the bathroom every day, sometimes twice. I felt like my body adapted well to the change in diet. Elaine's system did not fare so well. I noticed that she had **not** spent much time in the bathrooms and I had to ask her if she was all right. We're not shy on sharing our bowel habits, so she told me that she had not pooped in four days, and that she had not even had a twinge. Here I am munching and dumping like a madman for our first four days, and she hadn't even gone yet! Five, six then seven days pass, and I ask her again how her pooper was working, and she still hadn't gone!!! I was aghast, I looked at her and she didn't seem too troubled by this whole situation. She was a trooper, she kept on partying with me, seemingly, without a care in the world. I'm telling you, I would have become very familiar with German proctology after two days! In the meantime, I am blowing her out of our room at night with my gas, it was an awesome display of both power and smell. I know that when the smell of your own fart brings tears to your eyes, that it must be hell on your partner. Night number nine was the night, a date to live in infamy. We were in a hotel room near Munich, when the call came. I sat, waited and listened to one of the longest bowel movement sittings in history. She let it rip and emerged a very happy, lighter person. I read in the morning newspaper that the entire plumbing system of Bavaria was backed up; but there was relief in the eyes of the one who wasn't.

I mentioned cheese earlier and there is still a running debate in our family regarding the effects of cheese. Does it help promote the movement or does it inhibit the flow? My wife and daughter insist that cheese stops you up, but my mom and I feel otherwise. You see, they both have strong arguments in their favor. My mom flat out says that she shits down her legs and pants after eating cheese, while Elaine and Amber remain stopped up for days. I'm just a normal guy who is caught in the middle of dump wars. In my own defense, I take a great dump after eating pizza loaded with cheese.

I have another constipation story you may enjoy. Elaine and I took another vacation, this time with our daughter, who was about thirteen years old at the time. We stayed in the U.S. this time, probably because Elaine didn't want to smell any Brat farts. We flew down to stay at Disney World and to take a cruise on the Big Red Boat. The first five days were spent on land and we had a great time, except that the Amber had not pooped since we left. Here we go again. I just can't grasp this concept of not pooping regularly. My mom has Irritable Bowel syndrome, and that's okay, because anything labeled a syndrome, is serious enough for me to let it alone. But, for a healthy, thirteen year old who was walking with us about 4 miles a day, eating good meals, riding rides and sliding down water slides, (Oh, I may have come up with the problem), and not to be able to take a nice, healthy dump; I just can't imagine. I guess this is an inherited problem. So we leave Disney World after five days and head for the boat, and a four day cruise.

Day seven rolls around and she is feeling miserable, we had to take action. We already had her on those patches that prevent seasickness, and she didn't react well to those. She was seeing double and hallucinating; reminding me of my college days. We took her to the ship's doctor and he told us that some people have those reactions to the patches. We didn't bring up the constipation, because we felt we had that under control. We went for the old reliable, Ex lax. They carried it in the ship's grocery store. She was very embarrassed and refused to take the Ex Lax, and she fought us all the way, but it was in the middle of the eighth night when she gave in. She woke up Elaine and asked her for an Ex Lax. Elaine didn't turn on the light, but picked up the Ex Lax from the table, tore off a piece and handed it over to the Amber. It wasn't until the next morning that I discovered that Elaine had actually tore off six squares, not one! By the end of the afternoon, the poor little shit was running for the toilet constantly, afraid to leave the cabin, hallucinating, seeing double and shitting all over the place. It's funny, she has never expressed a desire to go on another cruise again.

On a side note, I did have a small poop problem of my own in that cabin. Our maid left those little chocolate mints on our pillows every night. I fell into bed with Elaine one night in somewhat of a drunken stupor and woke up to quite a scene. You see, I had forgotten to remove the mints from our pillows, and I managed to roll around so much in the bed, that the mints must have come unwrapped. I got up, stretched and looked down at our sheets, and to my horror, it looked as if I had shit all over the bed! There was brown patches, clumps and streaks everywhere. Elaine looked around her and jumped out of bed and screamed. She too, thought she had spent the night in a bed full of shit! There was a small knock on our cabin door, and there was the maid, ready to clean our room. She didn't speak English very well, but I still tried to tell her that it was chocolate, not poop, that was smeared all over the sheets. I should have pulled a Bill Murray, (Carl, the assistant groundskeeper), from Caddyshack, and put a piece in my mouth. I will never forget the look on that poor maid's face. We left her an extra special tip at the end of the voyage.

We are dog lovers and it would be hard to write a Big Book of Bowel Movements and not include a few anecdotes about our hounds. We currently have three dogs and all of them, including our cat, sleep in our bed every night. On a side note, Elaine and I feel that our dogs are better than most people we meet and are definitely part of the family. Dogs do have a few problems with constipation, but not many. Our dogs try to pick up scraps of paper or whatever they can get, and sometimes it comes back to bite them on the butt. One of our dogs must have eaten a large napkin or small towel, because she came walking into our living room with this hurt, wounded look on her face, and it took us a minute to figure out what was wrong. When she turned around, we saw half a rag sticking out of her little butt hole, and it looked painful. I think she was more embarrassed than anything. She was one happy dog after we yanked it out of her butt. Now that is a constipation story.

Constipation is a monster who rears it's ugly head on occasion. I am one of the lucky ones, who doesn't have to fight this beast very often, but for those of you who do, rest assured that I am out there rooting for you all the way.

Chapter Three

The Mouse Is Poking His Nose Out!

This expression is near and dear to me. I don't remember exactly when and where it originated, but I have a good idea. I was waiting tables in a San Diego restaurant during my college days, when I was asked one day to help train a new waiter. I immediately liked this charming fellow, not because of his restaurant prowess, but because he loved to talk about bowel movements. Jake Stub and I go way back and remain good friends to this day. I believe Jake and I came up with "the mouse" saying, and it has stuck ever since.

I know I am working on a great dump when I feel "the mouse poking his nose out." If you haven't figured it out yet, I'm referring to the act of working a dump to the point of near or semi near emergence. Now there are a couple of things I have to explain. "Working a dump" is just what the name implies, work it. I don't recommend this technique for everyone, especially inmates, because this technique requires huge sphincter control. When I can, I work my dumps every morning. As I sit here writing this, I am working my dump. I can feel it

work it's way through my system and if I wanted, I could head into the bathroom

right now, spend a few minutes reading and let it rip. There is nothing wrong with

this technique, believe me there are plenty of you out there who purposely head

into the bathroom way before a dump's maturity, just to catch up on some reading,

or to get away from the kids for awhile. More power to you, I'm just explaining

what works for me. I tend to let the dump come down the shoot a little further

than most. I realize I'm gambling, but life is short. There are positives and

negatives to using the mouse technique in dumping. A huge positive is that when

I head into the john, I am ready to complete the mission immediately, you know,

to deposit the payload on it's target. I go in, sit down, and let it blast out. If the

stool is fairly firm and I have worked it to good compactness, it usually leads to

an extra clean wipe; another huge positive. What I mean by compactness, is that I

have brought the mouse to the door, but haven't let him out. Every time I push

him back, it compacts the poop, and compact poop tends to be a cleaner, more efficient dump. I have to tell you, these positives are huge, I mean a good clean dump, great volume, quickly finished with little or no toilet paper; this is my idea of heaven on earth.

There are a few negatives about the mouse theory. The all time worst scenario is when I work a dump too long and the feeling goes away. I admit it, I sometimes get greedy when working my dumps, and I should learn from my mistakes. Have you ever worked your dump too long, or just waited too long to go, and the feeling goes away? It is a bummer. When it's there, go for it, don't screw around trying for more. It's like in baseball, when you try to stretch a double into a triple, don't do it unless you are certain to slide into third safe. I have done this, and when I do, I spend the rest of the day where it went and how can I get back that loving feeling. I don't wear underwear and I haven't for thirty three years, since high school. Skid marks are my enemy, and I have to watch out for them on a daily basis. I have to be very confident in my dumping abilities to both work the mouse and, not wear underwear. Depending on your marital status, and I say to this to all the women out there, coping with a proud dumper can be challenging in the best of times, but your men do love you for it. Skid marks are either something you accept, or something you desperately try to hide. My wife knows my underwear status and almost expects to see the skids when she loads the washing machine, but I will admit, that if I carelessly throw my pants on the floor with the inside crotch with skid marks up; that I will play the sensitive husband and turn my pants face down. I don't think skid marks are anything to be ashamed of, it is result of either poor mouse management, or a flu bug coming on mixed in with a little diarrhea. I think it was about a year ago, when I was at work and I let the mouse come out too far. I work in a real estate office with tight quarters and only one bathroom. I was answering phones when the mouse made a mad dash for my exit, and I couldn't stop him. I waddled my way into the bathroom with my cheeks clenched together, but I was too late. I pulled my pants down and the inside of my pants looked like a chocolate factory! I have been in that position before, so I didn't panic. The secret was to completely clean out the brown goo with wet paper, and as luck would have it, there was a wad of those multifold towels sitting on the bathroom sink. You can't use toilet paper in this scenario, it would turn to mush after wetting it. If this had happened at the end of the day, I would have done some minor damage control and gone home, but it was early in very long day. I knew I had to thoroughly soak my pants if I had any chance to last the day. I also knew that there was a huge mess in between my cheeks that needed attention. I had a few options here, one was to use an entire roll of toilet paper in hopes of cleaning it all up, or I could use plan B. Plan B is a little used option I use in only dire wiping situations. I wait to wipe, and flush the toilet a few times. This is critical because I will be dipping my hand into the toilet water and I want it clean.

After I see that the toilet water is clear, clean and sparkling, I wad up some toilet paper, dip it into the water and proceed to cleanup the mess that's stuck to my ass. This may seem like a radical move, but it works. I cleaned up my butt first, then moved on to the pants. I looked down into my pants, and it looked like a soft chocolate bar had melted in my pants! I took the multi fold towels, dipped them into the water and proceeded to wipe out my pants. I figured that I could handle sitting on a wet crotch for a few hours, I had done it before and I will do it again. It only took about a half an hour to realize my massive cleanup plan had not worked. I knew then how Exxon felt after the Valdez crisis in Alaska. The problem was that I rushed the cleanup. You have to do a thorough job when confronted with this problem, or you'll pay for it later, and I did. I noticed a putrid smell emanating from my pants, as I sat at my desk. By this time, the office was full of people. I retreated once again to the bathroom to check out the situation that was brewing in my pants, and to my horror, the poop stain had set into my light khaki pants, and bled through to the outside! The outside of my pants looked like I had sat on a melted Butterfinger candy bar. It wasn't just a little spot, but a huge spot the size of a tennis ball. I finally had to give up, the clean up plan had not worked. I made some lame excuse and decided to leave. I actually placed a piece of cardboard under my ass while I drove home. The car smelled like old, dried out poop. I don't have to tell you how bad those skid marks were.

What amazes me about skid marks is how long they can be, inside your pants. I just looked in a pair of sweats I wear around the house, and I have marks ten inches long. My butt crack isn't that long! I have also noticed that sometimes the entire side of the toilet seat is covered . Maybe I need to reevaluate my dumping procedure, but I tell you, it has worked like a charm for fifty six years, and I'm not about to change now. I can put up with a few poop stains once in awhile, as long as I can take an immaculate dump on a daily basis. Don't get the impression that every pair of pants I own are caked with poop, they're not, and in fact, only a small percentage of my pants end up with skid marks, and I'm proud of that. My wife hates it when I come down with a case of the Gout. You see, the quickest way to rid your self of the Gout is to take medicine that cleans out your system. The problem is that when it takes hold, the crap flows out your system at an alarming rate, causing the worst skid marks imaginable.

This goes unsaid, but I won't try to work the mouse when I'm suffering from diarrhea! The results are catastrophic. I have a hot tub in my house and I try to take a tub once or twice a day, it relaxes me. My problem is that when I take a tub in the mornings, the dump, the mouse, the excitement and the anticipation all go away. I don't think the mouse likes hot water. I understand that the sphincter has to shut down tight when submerging, but why does the mouse have to run for the hills? He sometimes won't show up again for hours or even the next day. The mouse has his own way and if you screw with the mouse, he will make you pay.

Just yesterday, I took a tub and it was a cold morning, but sometimes like a junkie, I didn't stop to think about the consequences for my actions. I went for the quick high, the soothing hot tub, without even stopping to give the mouse any consideration. Well, I paid the price. It was noon when I began worrying about my daily dump. I am not a coffee drinker, so I didn't go for the pseudo stimulation. I am a staunch believer in the pure bowel movement, with no artificial stimulators. I don't have a problem with those of you who use and abuse the coffee aspect in stimulating a bowel movement, but if you were a member of the World Bowel Movement Association, coffee would be cause for disembowelmovement.

The mouse started poking his nose out, like the groundhog in Punxatony, around 1:30 in the afternoon. I think the mouse was trying to tell me something, because I actually had to strain a bit to get it out and into the bowl. That reminds me of an interesting bit of trivia I read recently. Do you know the biggest cause of brain hemorrhages? It is straining on the toilet while taking a dump. I think I heard Skully on the X-Files say this also. I felt those veins in my temples bulging out as I tried to pinch out a pooplet, and although I did, I knew the mouse was trying to teach me a lesson. I will definitely take a tub after my dump in the morning.

You are probably thinking that I am a complete nut, and you're right. I do take chances by working the mouse, but the pros outweigh the cons. I have perfected my system and it works well for me, but it may come back to bite me on the butt in my older years. I figure I'm already destined for Depends and plastic bed sheets, so what the hell.

Chapter Four

The Closet Pooper

This is a subject I wasn't too familiar with until I married Elaine. I am a very open and sharing person, even about my dumps. I still try to coax her into the bathroom to admire my work, but she doesn't fall for it anymore. The honeymoon must be over. Elaine and our daughter Amber, are what I call "closet poopers". They don't talk about it, they do it private and most times hold it beyond belief, just to avoid a public bathroom.

I think there are many of you out there that feel that a bowel movement is a bane, something you have to do, a necessary evil. I truly feel sorry for you. A good bowel movement should be treated as a gift, to be revered and celebrated like a special occasion. I'm sure there are ancient civilizations who had huge celebrations of dump worship. They probably had to sacrifice a dump princess to their God's, to insure great bowel movements for the year to come. Taking a dump is a release of negative things. Taking a good dump is like hitting a bucket of golf balls. There are times in the business world when I want to beat somebody to a bloody pulp, but I realize that behavior isn't accepted in our society, so one way I take out my frustrations and let out all my negative energy, is on the driving range. With every swing, I release a little more of that negative energy, until I have hit enough balls to feel good about myself again. I don't mean to get psychoanalytical on you here, but it works. Taking a great bowel movement is basically the same thing. Your body is full of negative ions, and when you get the chance, the opportunity and the privilege to release that negative energy, you do it with gusto and delight.

Taking a dump in front of someone can be traumatic, even for those of us at the bottom of the evolutionary scale. Take for example when us guys have to take a dump in a public bathroom and the door is missing! Taking a dump, sometimes isn't a good look for many people. The grimacing and contorted look on one's face doesn't paint a pretty picture and won't endear you any closer to your loved one, so I can understand if somebody needs their space once in awhile. How many happily married people are out there who still haven't seen their spouse take a dump? I'd guess millions. My wife still insists on closing the door and yells at me when I enter while she is doing the dirty little deed.

Elaine also tells me that a closet pooper is very embarrassed about pooping in public. I've seen her hold a dump beyond recognition, just to avoid using a public bathroom. She tells me that some women will sometimes flush the toilet in public, just to camouflage the sound of turds hitting the water. I don't know first hand, but I imagine dumping protocol to be quite different in a women's room than in the men's. I find this hilarious, absolutely unbelievable, but she is my wife and I will stick by her.

Most of the time, I don't have a problem with taking a dump with the door open. There are many times when I'll be relaxing on the toilet, while Elaine sits at her vanity, just around the corner from me, and hold on a perfectly good conversation. I am not immune from taking a dump in private. I'll retreat to private dump mode if I know a tough wipe is coming or if I have skid mark damage control to perform. Until we married, Elaine never talked about bowel movements, and I think the way your were brought up has a lot to do with how you act and react to the dump subject. I think everyone's family has their little code words for pee and poop. The old classic is number one and number two. Who came up with this? It makes no sense whatsoever, what do the numbers question mark, like I mentioned earlier, my dad had his funny quirks. He called taking a dump, "going big". If this isn't the strangest name for taking a dump, I don't know what is. He also loved to take his dumps in the dark. I'd walk by his bathroom late at night and of course the door was open. There he'd be, this huge hulking man, sitting there in the dark, with is ripped briefs clinging to life around his ankles, and to top it off, our cat P.G. would be sitting on his lap! Oh yes, I came from a pretty normal family. Our cat P.G. (Pussy Galore, from a James Bond movie), would come running every time he stepped into the bathroom. That is warped, I'm sorry. So there he would be, just sitting there in the dark and he'd say, " Hi Kel", come on in, my "Big's" don't smell, in fact, they smell like strawberry ice cream". To this day, there are many unanswered questions about his bowel movement habits. Why would he always take a dump in the dark? What was he hiding from? Was he afraid of dumping in the light? Maybe he had some rare form of albinoism, where his dumps couldn't take the light. Maybe his sphincter only opened at night, and now that I think about it, he couldn't even turn around to admire his work, unless he turned on the lights after wiping. And where did the strawberry ice cream come from?

I wish I had him back to ask those questions, but for now, I'll just postulate. I feel I'm lucky, I was raised in an open family atmosphere. I have two older bothers, so my poor mom had to put up with a lot. I can't imagine how many dumps she had to stare at before flushing. I was always a flusher, but my brother's always left their handiwork behind, to be admired. My mom has said for years, that if she had it to do over again, that she would have raised dogs. Speaking of dogs, I now have five dogs and they, like P.G. the cat, do enjoy coming in while I take my dump. I wonder what they think when I wheel around to wipe myself. They must wonder why they don't use toilet paper to clean themselves, and why they are left to lick themselves clean. I think there are times when my dogs care who is watching them as they squat in their yards. I have five dogs, and sometimes they get shy when they are dumping in the yard with the whole world watching them. How can you be shy, when you are taking a dump in the middle of the front yard with all the neighbors watching? What a bummer it must be, to be a dog and a closet pooper. My dogs love to visit me when I take my dumps. It must be an animal thing, maybe they feel I'm communing with them, or that I am on their level or something. I just think they like the smell of my dumps.

I think we all agree that your upbringing is a huge factor with your outlook on taking dumps. My wife tells me that bowels, poop, crap or anything else along those lines were never spoken of in her home, growing up. She does tell me that the old reliable number system; number one and number two were used. At least she had that going for her. I feel sorry for her, but it just makes me appreciate her even more to see the enormous strides she has made in this facet of her life. She now lets me know when she has taken a stellar bowel movement, and I think that is the cornerstone of any great marriage.

Our daughter, Amber, still has some work to do in the closet pooper phase of her life. She is incredible, she will hold a perfectly good dump for hours, just to avoid the public bathroom. She tells me it isn't the hygiene or cleanliness of the bathroom that scares her off. She just gets embarrassed when she knows, that other people know, that she is taking a dump. I try and tell her that it is simply a bodily function that all human beings have to perform, and that it is nothing to get embarrassed about. She won't buy it. You should see her face when we are in A public place and she has to go. She gets this weird, sort of scared and confused look on her face, and won't say a word. I think back on all the Disneyland trips we took, and it must have been hell for her. I'll give you a good example of how advanced her closet poop mentality is. She came out last Christmas for a visit, and she called some old friends to get together. She took off one night about 9 o'clock to drive over to her friends house. She felt the mouse poking his nose out on the way over, and knew she was going to have to go. No big deal right? So she takes a dump at her friends house and gets on with her evening. Nope, she got to her friend's house, stayed about ten minutes, made up some excuse, and headed back home. Is that crazy or what? Granted, she had been stopped up for about five days, had some Ex-Lax in her system, and was a little worried about the fallout afterwards, but to drive home another half hour just to use her own bathroom, that is the true definition of a closet pooper. She told us she almost had to pull over on the side of the road to take her dump. That would have cured her of her closet mentality real fast. Elaine and I saw a little kid on the side of the freeway about a year ago, with his pants down to his ankles, taking a dump, while his parents tried to shield him from the onlookers.

I got a good laugh at that scene. I bet that kid will grow up to be just as warped as me.

The closet pooper isn't a good thing, but I realize there are other factors at work here. We can go back to that great philosophical debate on what factors develop the personality; heredity or environment? I think we can apply both of these principles to the closet pooper.. My wife is a perfect example of how one can spend their childhood hidden behind a veil of silence and emerge into an open, sharing person about her dumps. There is hope you all of you closet poopers out there. Our daughter is even making progress. She called to tell me that she has a new style to taking a dump, and it is working brilliantly. When she is at home, she takes off all her clothes to take a dump! She dumps in the nude! Is that hysterical or what? Hey, whatever works, right?

Chapter Five

The Setting

Many of us in our daily lives come across some pretty strange and beautiful places to take a bowel movement. There are of course, the familiar, comfortable spots that always make us feel at home. I'm sure that if we could make every alien bathroom more like ours at home, that the world would be a better place to live. How many of us have had to take a great dump, and we knew it was a great dump, but when we entered the awkwardness of unfamiliar surroundings; we just couldn't get it done.

The home dump is of course, the Cadillac of dumping spots. There are many factors that go into the setting that we take for granted. We have the familiarity of the toilet seat, the size of the bowl, the depth of the toilet water, the correct flushing sequence, the toilet paper's quality and where the refills are kept. There is of course, the lighting, reading material and last but not least, the time factor, there are no limits at home.

When at home, the toilet seat is either up or down, but the important thing is that we know **who** has been on the seat. Just look around you, there are some pretty scary looking characters that share our world with us, and to think we sometimes have to place our sweet cheeks where these strangers have placed theirs; well, it scares the hell out of me. Sure, you have those seat covers, or "ass gaskets", as I call them, but I don't ever seem to use them. I probably will as I get older, but for now, I guess I just pull my pants down, spread my cheeks and cast my fate into the wind. At home, we can just set the seat back down, and rest assured there aren't any creepy crawlies living on the edge of the bowl. How about those times you go into a public bathroom to take a dump, and the entire seat is covered with pee! Or there isn't a seat at all! For you women out there, that is something we men have to deal with all the time. Is it so tough to lift the seat when you take a pee? Have some common courtesy for God's sake. The toilet seat can of course, have it's quirks. I have a seat at home that has a screw loose, so I know that I can move to my right without a problem, but that sometimes when I go to my left, the seat will lift up and resist. This is important, this is the advantage of crapping on your home turf. This is the ultimate in home field advantage. There are also seats that stick to your butt, and I don't know why. My wife cleans our toilets on a regular basis, but sometimes afterward, my butt cheeks will stick to the toilet seat. The seat will actually rise up with my butt, as I get up from taking a dump. I feel like David Copperfield, doing a levitating trick. The seat always surprises me when it loses it's grip and goes slamming back down.

The size of the toilet seat is important, you know where you stand on your home turf, but there are some odd seats out there. Have you ever rushed into an unfamiliar toilet, dropped your pants and sat down on a toilet that was designed for a three year old? I'm not that big of a guy that needs an extra wide girth toilet seat, but there are some seats that make my butt feel like the size of Toledo. How about the all time favorite toilet seat debacle; when I sit myself down onto the toilet and my ass lands in the water! You'd think after all these years I'd learn to look before I sit, but no, I still manage to pull this one off once in awhile. I thought all toilet seats were standard, but I guess I'm wrong. I am homeowner, in my mid-fifties and I can honestly say that I have never bought a toilet. Maybe

the time is ripe, I may be able to add another chapter to this reading extravaganza.

The temperature of the toilet seat can make or break a good dump experience.

A warm seat, but not too warm (too much warmth on a toilet seat breeds

familiarity), can be a soothing factor, that allows for a stress free movement. A

cold seat makes me pucker up like a duck's ass in water, but I don't mind it much.

If I had my choice, Id go for a fresh, cold seat over a warm one. I'm not into the

fancy toilet seats, but there are some real doozies out there. There are padded

seats, carpet covered seats, and the strangest toilet seat I've encountered, was a

seat my brother Mike and I had to buy for my mother. She was having troubles

getting up and down to take a dump and to pee, (women use the toilet seat to do

both), so we went to a medical supply store and bought her a toilet seat. This seat

was beautiful, it was made of hard plastic and it attached to the bottom of her

toilet with a vise-like screw. The seat was about ten inches thick and had metal

hand grips on either side to help with pulling yourself up and down. It sat on her toilet, and I felt like a champion. I was jealous, I mean, to have metal hand grips for each arm, that is perfect. I could have used that seat, and in fact as I remember it now, I had a doctor recommend one to me after an ankle surgery last January. I'll tell the story in the last chapter, but just to wet your whistle; I blew my knee out while taking a dump.

I didn't realize it until I saw it on an episode of "Married with children", but there are different sizes to toilet bowls. Al Bundy was putting in a toilet out in his garage and he was explaining to Bud about the ultimate in toilet bowls. It seems his father had owned a particular brand that was the best made. Al Bundy took his bowel movements seriously didn't he? My hat is off to him. I now take a quick look at toilet bowls when I go into a home improvement store. There are all types of sizes, shapes and colors. I grew up thinking that all toilet bowls were standard. My father Larry should have taught me better, but then again, Larry thought a tool set was comprised of a screwdriver and a hammer. I can understand why there are different sizes of toilets, but is bigger better? Or is it the workmanship? I probably need to examine this topic a little better.

I have a toilet at my office that really pisses me off. I think we can all agree that one of the major goals of wiping, is to not have your hand end up in the toilet water. Well, the bowl at my office is so shallow, that my hand always seems to end up in the water. How far is too far, to have to raise your ass to get a good wipe angle, without dunking your hand into shitty water? What is the purpose of a shallow bowl? I suppose it could save water, and yes, I understand that, but the toilet bowl is not where we should be conserving water.

Flushing should be one of those things, that while living in the technological world, we should never have to worry about, but I do. I can't tell you how many times I have changed the handle, float, chain and the entire guts of one of my toilets at home, and it still doesn't flush properly. We live in a world in which we can pinpoint a target from thousands of miles away, send a missile, and it lands within a few inches of it's target; but we can't invent a toilet that flushes perfect every time. Have you ever gone to a hardware store to buy a replacement part for your toilet, and you see forty different companies selling the same parts? All those companies are making money, so that tells me that someone out there has convinced the government, that it would be wrong to invent a maintenance free toilet. Yes, I believe there is a toilet conspiracy.

My wife claims that I need to know how to flush our problem toilet. What, you push down on the metal handle and it should flush everything down the toilet, only to refill with clean, bright, gleaming water. Mine does not work that way. There are about five different scenarios when I flush my problem toilet. One is that it flushes perfect the first time, no problem. This occurs every leap year. The second is that the handle gets so stuck that it won't flush a tall. Third is that it will flush, but all the toilet paper just floats on top and goes nowhere, while the rest of the bowl drains. Fourth is when the water swishes around but nothing goes down, and the last scenario is when I get so pissed off that I yank the top off the toilet and put my hand in the water and manually flush the toilet. I have always wondered how no poop or anything sneaks into the water in the chain-float area. It has to sneak in there once in a while. Let's put it this way, I wouldn't drink that water on a bet.

I can say that I am not a shy dumper. If I have to go, I go. I don't analyze it or think about holding it until I get to familiar surroundings, I just go. I do have a problem with some public bathrooms. The absolute worst is when the only open stall has no door! I was never in the military and I hear they had to dump, pee and shower together, but to take a dump in public without the privacy of a door, well that, is just plain uncivilized. I takes a lot of gumption for many of us to take a dump at home with the door open, but to pull it off in front of total strangers, that takes balls. The public bathroom scene is ugly for us men. There are grunts, farts, groans, gas emissions, sounds and facial expressions that best be kept within the confines of a closed room. I'll dump all day long with twenty people waiting for my stall without a problem, as long as I have a door I can close. I don't care if there isn't a lock, I can always prop my foot up against the door for protection. While I'm broaching the subject, where do all the bathroom stall doors go? Does someone steal them, and if they are, what would you do with a stall door? I guess you could use it to replace the one that is missing from your favorite public bathroom. Somewhere out there is a huge cache of bathroom stall doors, and one day I'll find it.

It is sometimes easy to get intimidated when dumping in a public bathroom. It seems every time I sit down to do the deed, there is some other guy one stall over just blasting away. The whole nine yards here, farts as long as your arm, grunts as loud as a bullhorn, and the smell is horrific. I put together a pretty good package when I take my show to the public toilet, but it seems that some of these guys save up all week, just so they can grandstand in public. I'd go head to head with any of jokers on a day to day basis, then we'd see who would come out on top.

The workplace dump is complex in many ways. The location of the bathroom plays an integral role in your dump habits at work. I work in a real estate office where everyone's desk is within earshot of one another's, as well as the bathroom. There is some sorry bastard that has his desk right next to the men's room. My wife and I have seniority, so we station ourselves far from the action. First off, let's get it out in the open on whether or not you are comfortable taking a dump in your workplace toilet. I hit on this topic a little earlier when I mentioned that my wife and daughter are closet poopers. This definitely applies to this situation. Get over your fear, take the first step to financial and bowel freedom and find peace with your office toilet. I've been in some very nice work-place toilets, and in fact been very envious, but our toilet leaves nothing to the imagination. A toilet, sink and a wad of toilet paper. There is a guy in our office, I swear, that when he comes out of the bathroom, the whole office can tell what he ate the night before. Sure, our office manager places a can of foo foo spray in the john, but it just makes the shitty smell, sweeter. It's truly horrible.

Another quirk about my office, is the women's bathroom directly adjoins our conference table, where we hold our weekly sales meeting. I can't help but laugh whenever a woman gets up during our meeting to take a pee, or on very rare occasions, take a bowel movement. You can definitely hear the flow, the unrolling of the toilet paper, the flush and the obligatory washing of the hands. Now that takes balls, to walk out of there, knowing 25 people just listened to your every move. The women have to know, but I won't tell, I can't ruin a good thing.

Europe is an adventure in dumping. Elaine and I took the Amber and her friend to Europe a few summers ago for a six week camping tour. We saw ten countries in six weeks, and took dumps in some pretty interesting places. Looking back on it, I should have packed some decent toilet paper, and did the bear in the woods routine, but I was with three women, and that was an adventure in itself. First of all, Europe hasn't discovered a toilet paper that actually wipes. Their toilet paper does a nice job of smearing, and that's about it. You talk about some gnarly skid marks! I guess I should have broke down and brought some undies, bought I took my chances. I have news for the great continent, the old world; we here in America have toilet paper that actually wipes your ass clean! Please don't get me wrong, I love Europe, and have visited three times now, but I will probably start bringing a few rolls next time.

The campgrounds in Europe were awesome, they all had bathrooms, showers, bakeries, restaurants, bars and sometimes, discos. What they lack in toilet paper, they certainly kick our butt in the campground department. E-mail me if you're planning a trip, I'll give you some great spots to camp. The worst toilet we encountered was in a campground on the coast, across the bay from Venice, Italy. I walked into the bathroom and saw what looked to be a normal, stand up urinal that us guys see in every public bathroom. The problem was that I didn't see a toilet anywhere and I had to take a dump, and a mushy one at that. As I inspected the urinal closer, I noticed two indentations in the porcelain, on the floor, that resembled foot prints, but the footprints were pointing out toward me! Mmm, I thought, and then it dawned on me, that this was the toilet for dumping and peeing! You had to drop your pants, turn around, place your feet in the molds, and let it fly. There wasn't even a bowl of water at the bottom, just a screen to catch the debris. The hardest part wasn't overcoming the sheer fear of this exercise, but I kept wondering how far I had to lean backwards, so that I wouldn't drop my load right into my shorts. Plus, I had the pee thing to think about, who knew which direction that was going to go! Put all this together with the fact that there were guys walking in and out all the time, watching me try to perform this circus trick, well, it was all pretty exhausting. I needed a drink after that fiasco. I can't imagine what my face looked like; part fear, grimace, embarrassment, but a little exhilaration too. The only good aspect to this experience was the power of the flush. I pushed down on the button on top, and whoosh, with the power of a dam being released, all my efforts were washed away, down the drain. If I could only get that kind of pressure at home, I'd probably sell tickets.

Have you ever been at someone's house and had to take a dump? I think we have all experienced that. Elaine has a line of defense in our bathrooms, it's called Glade air freshener. It seems our friends don't have a problem taking a dump in our bathroom and that makes me feel like the good host, There are those homes that you have to think twice about dumping in. Elaine will flat out hold her movement, she will not take a dump in someone else's house. I think this is crazy and I tell her so, but she refuses to give in to rationality. Taking a dump is something every human being does, we shouldn't be ashamed of releasing our bodily waste, wherever and whenever the occasion arises. I will admit that taking a dump in someone's house can be a little nerve racking. You hope and pray it is a clean dump with an easy wipe, (thus one flush), and most important of all, no smell! Nothing can ruin the ambiance of a party worse than a little kid running out of the bathroom screaming, "someone just stunk up the bathroom". It reminds me of spending the night at a friend's house, as a kid. Remember how hard it was to get up in the middle of the night to take a pee, worrying about whether or not your friends parents would hear you. I would lay in the sleeping bag and hold it till I was blue in the face, just to avoid the possible embarrassment of being caught peeing. Pooping was out of the question, peeing was always the problem. Then, the ultimate decision was whether or not to flush. On one hand, if you flushed, you risked the wake up scenario with the noise, but if you did not you could get blamed for leaving pee in the toilet. This was a traumatic thing in my young life, but I'm glad to say that I have overcome that fear.

My dogs got it made. I have always had dogs and I have witnessed thousands of dog dumps. We currently have five dogs, and that is a lot of dog crap; but I do revel in the purity of their movements. They have no hang ups, no worries about wiping, skid marks, odor or even where to go. My dogs experience the ultimate, pure bowel movement on a daily basis. I watch as they wander out into the yard, smell around for a good, clean spot, squat down and let out the perfect bowel movement almost every time. Their butts are like those play dough machines that used to spit out those funny shapes. Why don't dogs need toilet paper? maybe we're in the wrong for using it. My dogs just snap off one dump after another, clean as a whistle, tapered at the end, decent odor, great consistency and no need for any toilet paper. It reminds me of an old joke, Why are turds tapered at the end? So your ass won't slam shut... My dogs are dumping marvels. They also have no shame as to who watches them, except on rare occasions. I can sit on my back deck and talk to them as they lay immaculate dumps, and it won't faze them a bit. I sometimes wonder if dogs aren't superior to humans, in the bowel movement scheme of things.

We can't forget one of the most important aspects of taking a dump, the reading material. I am in the minority here, but I really don't take reading material with me into the bathroom very often. This is due to the fact that I work the mouse, so that when I enter the bathroom to do the deed, I'm already at full strength when my cheeks hit the porcelain. There are millions of men out there who revel, who look forward to their own private time on the toilet. I have very little information regarding the female of the species and their reading habits on the toilet, if any, but I do know that I've never heard a woman say, "hey, pass me the sports page, I have to go pinch a loaf". The reading thing is a male trait and who knows where it came from. I'd trace it back to the caveman, but there wasn't a newspaper back then. Maybe they were scribbling their hieroglyphics on the side of the cave while they were taking a dump. I guess I'm doing about the same thing right now, wow, how man has evolved.

Surfer magazine was always at arms reach from the toilet as I grew up, and still is sometimes. It is an easy magazine to peruse while taking a dump, a somehow comforting publication to use as a dumping aphrodisiac. I think the colors of the magazine have a big effect. The magazine is predominantly blue and shades thereof, which lends itself to a soft, cool, comforting feeling; thus allowing the sphincter to loosen it's grip and let those turds slide on through like a surfer, in a gnarly twelve foot barrel at Pipeline. There are many analogies to made here, what between logs, tubes, water, etc., but I'll leave the sanctity of taking a bowel movement while reading Surfer magazine alone.

I think the sports page of the newspaper and Sports Illustrated fit into the bathroom very well. It is a male thing; you can take your time to study the statistics and you can plan out your television viewing schedule for the weekend. Whether you are at home or at work, sports reading gives you the excuse you need to spend those precious few extra minutes alone with your thoughts, on the toilet. It is a perfect fit for the bathroom. There are other books and magazines that also work well, but those are second rate, compared to sports pages. I am little strange, but I have a book on trivia sitting on my toilet, as well as a pen and paper; I get inspired while dumping.

Don't underestimate the importance of the setting when taking a dump. There are many factors that may distract us while we attempt to produce a fine bowel movement. I say don't let those factors spook you, if we remain focused, I think we can all produce stellar bowel movements anywhere, anytime. Next time you remodel the bathroom, keep your bowel movements in mind.

Chapter Six

Wiping

I wonder when man began wiping himself. I'm sure it was the woman who invented wiping, it only makes sense, they are the more civilized of the species. I could guess I could trace it back to the ancient Egyptians and the making of papyrus, (the early origins of paper). Or if you believe in aliens landing on earth in ancient times, then you would have to give them the credit; I mean after all, if they were so advanced, they had to know about wiping and then it taught it to the Incas or some other culture. One thing is for sure, wiping is a big part of anyone's day, and I treat it with respect. A wipe can make or break anyone's day.

My theory behind wiping is very simple, don't do it if you don't have to. I know I am a dreamer, but we have all had it happen a few times in our lives. I can remember those rare occasions in which I didn't need any toilet paper after taking a dump, and it has been awhile . Taking a dump underwater doesn't count, but it is a great feeling. Our dog Sunshine loved to go swimming in the river nearby, but she would always squat down low enough to take a dump under the rushing water. Now that is a wipe in it's purest form. The perfect wipe is has to coincide with the aligning of the planets and the Gods have to be watching over you, as you sit there and snap off the perfect bowel movement. Perfectly tapered at the end, great, solid consistency and perfectly smooth, as to slide through the anus and drop, without a splash, into the cool bowl of water. I know it when it happens, I feel it and yet I'm curious as to what would come off onto a sheet of toilet paper, if I was to wipe. How would life be, if every dump were the perfect dump, without having to use toilet paper. Imagine the trees we'd save; we'd probably help end global warming and reduce the greenhouse effect on our atmosphere if we never had to use toilet paper. Imagine all the rain forests we are diminishing daily, just so we can wipe our precious asses. I think we all use too much toilet paper, let's cut it down a square per wipe and let's see what happens.

Wiping is an art form, and there are many types of art in this world, so no one way is the correct way to wipe. Wiping is in the eye of the beholder. If my brother's bed sheets are any indication, he's doing his part to save the rain forests. His skid marks are impressive. I have actually used many different styles of wiping throughout my career. It is hard to categorize different wiping techniques, so I'll ramble on from the top of my head. My toilet note pads come in handy with this chapter. The "between the legs" technique, doesn't work for me, but I this is a popular wipe. Don't get me wrong, I'm not saying any one way is right or wrong, I'm not a wiping snob. If you have a particular style that works for you, stick with it, remember the old saying, "if it isn't broke, then don't fix it." The between the legs doesn't work for me because I like a good cheek spread before I go in, that is why I consistently use the "from behind" technique.

Wiping from the front, between the legs is a messy wipe for me. Now, I am speaking from a male's point of view here, I believe most women use this style for obvious reasons. The major problem I find with this style, is like I mentioned before, it does not let you spread your cheeks very wide and we all know that a good wipe requires a good ass spread. A lot does depend on your definition of a good wipe. Some are content to get most of the poop and then there is the other school of thought, that requires an absolute resolution to the problem. I fall into the second school of thought. I want to get up from the toilet, put on my pants, and with confidence, at anytime, scratch my ass and dig deep if need be, and come up with no skid mark. This is a purists way of thinking, but it also requires more work, time and patience. The problem I have with the between the legs wipe is two fold. One is that it is easy to get some poop on your hand or wrist, especially if the poop has crept up further than you think. Second, is that those of us with lots of anal hair, have a tendency to have a dingle berry problem, and the "betweener" tends to leave the dingle berries behind. I think most women use the betweener to do their business and that is fine, they definitely don't have the anal hair thing going, and if they do, I don't want to know them. I don't get the full cheek separation using this technique, but I may have overlooked some fine detail. There are times when I have been forced to use this technique and I have found that I had to get a huge rise off the seat, for full wipe capability. I also have found that his technique lends itself to leaving a trail on the sides of your cheeks, thus leaving two skid marks on your butt cheeks; one on the left and one on the right.

The other school of thought on wiping is coming in "from behind". This works well for me for many reasons. I am ambidextrous, which is huge, it means I can use my right or left hand with the same dexterity. When coming in from behind, it's easy for me to lift my cheek, (right cheek with right hand and left for left), and give my best effort to gather all the Klingons from rear to front, with one fluid motion. As I get older, I find that one wipe does not get the job done anymore. This brings me to the subject of how you grab the toilet paper. Do you wrap it around your hand a few times, or do you fold it into the palm of your hand neatly or like me, scrunch it up into a wad and securely place it in your hand. I like this technique because it allows me the freedom to dig a little deeper if need be. There is nothing worse than having your toilet paper slide off your hand during mid wipe, which raises another question. How far can you take your wipe before it is considered perverted? Is there protocol for this sort of thing? If Congress wants to convene and come up with type of recommendation, I would be happy to give them my views. If I have the time and feel the need, I go for the quad wipe. This wipe is the ultimate cleaner wipe. If I feel a messy, smeary bowel movement, then I bring out the big guns and pull off the quad. First I load up my right hand and come in from the right, not with the intention of getting everything in the middle. I then load up my left hand and repeat this procedure for the left side. The final two moves are down the middle, with the fourth taking on the mop up role, like a third string quarterback in a blowout football game.

An important aspect of the "behind wipe", is that my hand has something to rest on, something to help guide me down the dirt highway. My butt cheek is perfect to help steady my hand while wiping. It doesn't lend itself to many messy wipes and it allows me to take care of any dingle berries. Removing dingle berries can be painful. I try to grip the dingle berry with the toilet paper, but I always seem to pull out hair with the grab. This is a very delicate situation.

Another very important quality of the behind wipe is huge cheek spread capability. When I lift my right or left cheek off my seat, I am creating a Grand Canyon for my hand to glide through, it's a beautiful thing. While I'm on the subject, why was wiping an easier exercise when we were younger? Was it because we didn't care? Or was it a physical difference in our bodies. I guess when you are smaller, everything is smaller like your poops, sphincter and cheeks. I also remember that skid marks were not a childhood concern of mine; if I had them, who cared? I just took my pants off and threw them into the dirty clothes hamper and let my mom take care of it. I think I just hit on something significant. The reason why wiping and skid marks weren't a childhood concern, was because we didn't have to do our own laundry! We now do our own laundry and we don't care to deal with poopy pants or skid mark infested undies. My mother must have seen some pretty scary undies as we grew up. I grew up with two older brothers, so I can imagine the horror my mother had to face when laundry day rolled around. I suppose if I were still living with my mom, and she was doing my laundry, I wouldn't have a care in the world regarding my wipes or poop stains.

As I mentioned earlier, I sometimes wipe from both sides, using both hands. My brother Mike was even amazed to learn of this style. I know it is eccentric, but it gets the job done. Although I do almost everything left handed, I cover more ass space while wiping with my right hand, so you may want to give it a try going in from the opposite side, you might be surprised.

A few questions come to mind regarding accidents while wiping. What do you do when your hand accidentally slips while wiping, and you end up with poop on your hand? Or if your finger punctures the paper and ends up smack dab in the middle of poop? Do you sometimes smell it? Do you get up immediately to wash it off and leave the finish wipe for later? Do you go the full hot water and soap thing while your pants are down at your ankles and your dirty ass sticking out? Or do you wipe the poop off your hand with another wipe to temporarily get you into the finish wipe phase? Or the worst case scenario is just leaving the poop on your hand or finger while you finish taking your dump and wipe. This is a horrible topic, but shit happens. I want to come clean right now, this has happened to me, and not only once. First off, when it happens I get pissed off at the toilet paper. It has to be the paper's fault, I mean I have been wiping my ass now for over forty years, and to still have an accident like this happen to me, well, it's unacceptable. I blame the toilet paper. When I find a good toilet paper, I stick with it. I love these toilet paper commercials telling us the virtues of how soft the paper is on your ass.

paper is on your ass. I like soft toilet paper, but hey Mr. Whipple, I have never taken a dump, wiped my butt and said to myself, "Wow, that sure was soft toilet paper." I think those ads are geared more toward women, because they are wiping other more sensitive areas down there. I used to go to the store and buy the "On sale", brand of toilet paper, but I am older and wiser now and I feel that I can splurge a little and buy the paper that works best for me. It is important, when shopping for toilet paper, to comparison shop. It pays to read the fine print and compare. The two most important factors in choosing toilet paper are the number of sheets per roll, and the ply. You may find a pack of 48 rolls, but they might not compare to a pack of 36, depending on the number of sheets per roll. Take a calculator with you next time, you'll see what I'm saying. We need not even discuss the importance of ply, ply is the thickness of the paper. I like to go with the Price Club/Costco brand that has 40 or 60 rolls to a pack. For some perverse reason, I like walking through the store with one of those huge packages of toilet paper, sticking out of my basket. I think it says to everyone, " I take a lot of dumps, I use a lot of toilet paper, and I feel good about it.

I think your stance is a huge factor in creating the perfect wipe. Have you ever worn a pair of pants that were a bit too snug and when you dropped them to the ground to take dump, you couldn't get your feet to spread far apart? It's horrible. In those rare cases, I say "screw it", and take my pants completely off, spread my legs for a good, well ventilated, well separated wipe. No encumbrances produce the better wipe. Take my daughter Amber for example, she now takes all her clothes off when taking a dump and I am all for it. You can't get a good wipe if your feet are too close together. It's physics, your cheeks have to be spread apart as far as possible in order to achieve a good, clean wipe. I like the elastic sided pants, because they bundle up and make me look thinner when I wear a belt with them, but when it comes to "Go time", they loosen their grip and allow me the freedom to wipe. Wiping a sloppy poop is a complicated and sometimes tiresome exercise. I know when I have a sloppy dump coming, I can feel it in my bowels and I definitely feel it as the mouse moves on down. I know this dump will resemble a huge pile of pudding or wet cement. I don't work the mouse when I know a messy one is coming. In fact, I don't fool around with this one at all; I get into the toilet and get the job done before a massive problem develops. I swear, I have taken dumps in which I go down to wipe and poop will end up on my forearm! Or how about the times when you get up, there is poop on toilet seat? How does poop get from that small orifice to completely cover my butt cheeks or toilet seat? My ass must look like I pulled my pants down and sat in a huge, hot pile of mushy poop, completely covering both my ass cheeks. This amazes me, even as I write, I can't understand how this happens to a grown man.

I have a few different ways to wipe the sloppy dump. The first option I consider is to use damn near half a roll of toilet paper to get the job done. If I'm in a hurry, this won't work for me. I feel guilty using that much paper, but I have to do it sometimes. I have to admit that I still don't feel confident using this method. It seems that if I wipe myself eleven times, I could go in again and still get some poop or residue on the twelfth, and so on. What a vicious circle. The second option I consider depends on the days activities that lay before me. For example, If I am at the office and ready to head home and I have to take a messy dump, I won't do the half a roll thing, but instead, get the majority of the poop and save the rest for the comfort and familiarity of home. I admit, this lends itself to a whole lot of skid mark problems, but a little Tide always does the trick in the washing machine. The third wiping option I use on very rare occasions and I must say this is a bit on the weird and even abnormal side, is what I call the "Paper dunk" method. If I feel the mess is too much for even half a roll, then I go to my sure fire method of cleaning up my butt. Before I try to wipe, I flush the toilet as many times as needed to clear the water of any debris. This method should only be tried at home, behind closed doors. After the water has cleared

and I make sure there aren't any floaters, I wrap a huge chunk of toilet paper

around my hand, dunk it in the toilet water and not too deep, because too much

water can cause the toilet paper to disintegrate. I try to get about half the wad wet

and then I take it to my cheeks first and repeat the steps until I have covered all

the ground necessary . Yes, I know I sound like a lunatic, but it works and it pull

you out of a jam if you let it. I then immediately take my hands to the sink and

wash off very well with soap and water. I'm not a complete idiot.

The fourth and last of my wiping options is the shower. If I make it to the

bathroom too late and I know it, I don't even fool myself into thinking I can

salvage this wipe with paper. I take the dump, of which some is usually nestled in

my pants, and I say "Screw it." I take my pants off, throw them into the washer

and step into the shower to completely clean up my mess. I always hope

everything makes it down the drain. I know this sound drastic and it may sound

like I am always cleaning up my ass with showers and wet paper, but these really

are rare occasions, I promise. I know the shower scenario sounds drastic, but

drastic times require drastic measures. I get pretty embarrassed when I have to

use this method, and I try to pull it off without my wife figuring out what is

going on. The most important aspect is making sure there isn't any poop in the drain. She looks at me pretty weird when I get up in the morning, put on my comfy clothes to go in and work on the computer; and then half an hour later, I'm taking a shower, doing a load of laundry and have changed into different comfy clothes. I try to casually pass it off as just me being weird, but I think she has it figured out.

Have you ever had to do the mid day wipe? You know the one in which you didn't get all of it in the morning and you know there is still some residue between your cheeks all warm and mushy. Since moving from California up here to Washington ten years ago, I haven't had this problem nearly as often. I attribute this to the cooler climate, you see, I think warmer days contribute to the residue between your cheeks becoming mushy and runny. Anyway, this is a most satisfying wipe. Number one, it is quick and easy. Number two, it completely resolves the problem in one quick wipe. I usually look at the toilet paper after this wipe because I'm curious how much residue I left behind from my morning wipe. I take this to heart, I strive to constantly better myself in the wiping aspect of my life, and If I see where I went wrong with my morning wipe, maybe I can improve on it next time. I wish all wipes were like the mid day wipe. There is also the question of how to wipe poop out of your pants, if you have no choice but to wear them out of the bathroom. This is a huge problem if you are in a work type environment and don't have the luxury of a shower nearby. A lot depends on the color of your pants and how they will show water. I have taken wet napkins and done a quick cleanup job before at work, but the water stain was too much and it spread through my pants, making me look like I just sat in a puddle of water. If this isn't done well, it can also leave an after smell that will follow you like the cloud around "Pigpen", in the Peanuts cartoon strip. If you are going with the wet napkin, do a thorough job and give yourself enough time to dry out at your desk or some other sitting position. The key is to get it all wiped out and to not rush yourself. I made the mistake of doing this with a light colored pair of pants. I rushed it and didn't get all the poop out of the pants. I realized later on in the day, but I had been walking around the office with a baseball sized poop stain that bled through my pants.

Wiping is a critical factor in life. We can all go through life taking huge, immense bowel movements, but if we can't finish the job properly, we're all lost. I think too many people rush through the job of wiping. If the wipe is done right, it can be just as satisfying as the dump itself. Don't hurry the wipe, embrace it.

Chapter Seven

The Dump

The dump is a mysterious creature. It comes in all sizes, shapes, and odors with an almost unlimited number of combinations. When I think of how many different combination possibilities there are, well, it just boggles my mind. For example, how many times have you taken an immense dump with no smell, while on the other hand, taken a pooplet dump that peeled the paint off the bathroom walls with it's stench. I have already taken us through a few factors that effect the dump, now let's delve into the subject of the actual bowel movement.

Dumps have a mind of their own at times. I don't understand how I can go four months straight, taking my daily, morning dump between 7 a.m. and 9 a.m., and then all of a sudden a dump shows up at 10 o'clock in the evening. I call this phenomenon a rogue dump. It comes without warning and comes on fast. There is something disturbing about having to get up from bed at night and take a dump! How about the dump that actually wakes you up from sound sleep? Where does that come from? I'm sure the food we ate had something to do with it, but to wake us up from sound sleep? Is nothing sacred?

Dumps also have a way of fooling us at times. How about the dump that comes on like gangbusters while we're driving or in some meeting, and it feels like it will shoot out of our ass that very moment, but when we make a mad dash for the bathroom, it disappears! That dump really pisses me off. I really try hard on that one, because I know it is there somewhere, but it refuses to come out and show itself. I heard somewhere, and I think it was "Skully", from the "X-Files", say, that most brain hemorrhages happen in the bathroom, and like "Mulder", I believe it. I have spent some pretty agonizing moments on the toilet, holding my breath until I hear my pulse and feel my temples throbbing, just trying to shoot out some little, insignificant turd. On the other hand, there are those dumps that start shooting out when I'm still three feet away from the porcelain. I guess I can think of some worse ways to die, and in fact dying while taking dump might not be so bad. I'd probably die as a martyr for bowel movement enthusiasts everywhere.

There are many aspects of the actual dump I wish to elaborate on, from the smell and consistency to the color. I might repeat myself from some other spot in this scholarly book on dumps, so I apologize now ahead of time. I tend to repeat myself sometimes, feel lucky I'm not drinking while writing. Dumps can be categorized much like jewelers categorize diamonds. You've heard it before, the four "C's"; color, carat, cut and clarity. I categorize dumps by the four "S's"; size, smell, shape and shade of color.

There is something about wiping I forgot to mention, so I'll go back a minute and discuss it. In my quest for the perfectly clean wipe, I have found myself digging a little deeper in order to make sure my wipe lasts all day. Now how far can I go? Is there a rule or protocol as to how far up the anus you can go with the finger, before it's considered perverted? You have to admit, there are times when you have to do it and whether or not you want to admit it, it actually feels pretty good. Don't get the idea I like to walk around with my finger up my ass all day, I don't, but you have to suck it up sometimes and do the dirty deed. Those mushy poops have a way of sneaking down on you in the most inopportune times, so why not think ahead, get the job done right and move on.

Bowel movements come in a variety of sizes, from the tiny jawbreaker size to the baby's forearm size. How versatile is that sphincter? The sphincter is much like the Panama Canal, it can let the huge tankers through with little room to spare and they also let the small sailboats glide on through. The main difference is that the Panama Canal doesn't shrink up to the size of a Corn nut after the tanker goes through. This is a marvel of biology, how the butt hole shuts down tight as a duck's ass in water, after every dump. Bowel movement length is also a factor I clump in with size. My wife measures farts by length, and I don't know why I'm bringing this up other than I think it's hilarious. I'll fart, look at her and ask her how long it was. She'll put her hands out, spread apart and say, "About this long." It gets me every time. She also has a way of telling me she has to take a dump. She'll tell me that she has a "stomach ache." For years I thought she actually had a stomach ache, but that wasn't the story. She was actually telling me that she had to take a dump. My stomach rarely hurts before I have to take a dump, so I don't know where that came from, but I'll accept it. Have you ever bought those "snakes", on the Fourth of July, where you light them and they squirm all over the sidewalk and then your parents yell at you for staining the sidewalk forever? Unfortunately, I have dumps that look just like those snakes. I

I know there is a problem with my diet, when the snake dump comes a calling. I recently had two teeth pulled and the friendly oral surgeon gave me a prescription for painkillers. As I mentioned earlier in the constipation chapter, when I get painkillers, I don't screw around, I take them and I take them as directed. I didn't take a dump for three days! I was proud of myself though, I have had a previous experience with Percodan and I knew the side effects were only temporary, so I hung in there waiting for the inevitable. I can't say that I wasn't a little worried, I was. As I laid around the house popping pain pills, I knew the beast was gathering from within. I hoped the poop would come to me in normal fashion; early morning, good volume, moderate smell with a good clean, smooth wipe. That was not to be. The first dump in three days was a Milk Dud dump! How can a body consume three days worth of food and only omit four little pooplets? That was my only dump on day four. I then started to freak out and cut back on my prescription. It seems to me it's like there are different turd making factories in your bowels. There's the small, family run factory that when asked, produce the very small, hard pooplet. Then there's the sloppily run factory that when given the order, produce a huge, runny product with putrid smell. This factory pays off the inspector in order to stay in business like the wise guys on the docks.

Then there is the factory that specializes in custom turds with various sizes, shapes and colors. They produce those turds that are shaped like animals, letters or even question marks. I've even had a dump that resembled an exclamation point! That is good work! The last but not least of the inside bowel turd factories, is the U.S. Steel of turd making companies. They deal in volume, and volume only. If I had to work for one of those companies, this is the one I'd choose, pure American, pure volume.

Of all the dumps, I think the pooplet is the most disappointing and tricky. It wouldn't be so bad if you knew the pooplet was coming, but it disguises itself very well. This dump is a real trickster. The pooplet disguises itself as a huge dump, with the pain in the bowels and all the other little telltale signs, but I know there is something wrong the minute I sit down on the toilet. I can tell there isn't anything down there to work on. It did it's job as a decoy, it got me to drop what I was doing, pull my pants down, and sit down on the toilet, and that is the perverse way the pooplet gets off. This crap has no conscience, no morals at all. This shallow, lowlife poop is probably down in the bowels laughing it up with all his poop buddies, but I am a competitive person at heart and I refuse to give in to this shallow, skeleton of a real poop. It's easy to let this ruin your day and I won't get up off my toilet until something has come out, and I don't care if it is the size of a raisin, or how hard I had to grunt, groan or push. I feel sanctified when I look down and this tiny, however significant turd, just lay there on the bottom of the bowl. If I die of a brain hemorrhage while taking a dump, I'll lay money on it now, the authorities find a pooplet at the bottom of my toilet bowl.

The pooplet is also a harbinger, a sign of either times to come or what has passed. It is a transition poop, either the beginning of a constipation phase or the ending of a sick, (pain pill), phase. Anyway I spell it, the pooplet dump is bad news. If the pooplet was a person, I'd see him as an ugly thug in torn clothes, wielding a knife in some dark, stanky alley. If you see him, you know there is trouble, run like the wind.

The dump that upsets me, but also amazes me, is the spaghetti dump. This dump is a curious animal. It gives no warning of a problem down in the poop factory, and in fact most times it comes out fine, but there are those rare occasions when the snake rears it's ugly, but very long head. I'm talking about the dumps that squirt out and seem to go on forever. You know, the one's that are so long they end up breaking apart in three places. The part that amazes me is that the

Dump is as long as a 747, but the distressing part is that it has the girth of a licorice whip. I sometimes wonder if there is a clog in the sphincter, maybe there is a peanut caught in the exit, or there is a jam in the sphincter opening. My dad, Larry, sold pipes, valves and fittings for forty years, I should know something about clogged pipes.

The dump I hate to bring up, but have to, is the sphincter splitting dump. There is a saying that " there is a fine line between pain and pleasure", well, that saying was invented while taking this dump. On one hand, it is a very satisfying bowel movement, with the girth and all, but it can also hurt like hell. It feels like you're pooping a baseball bat, but there is rarely any great length to this dump. I think this dump has a problem with texture or softness. Have you ever noticed that when you take this dump, it is usually hard as a rock? Why does this dump, above any other, have to be that hard? It would be great if you could push a button and control the texture of your dumps. For example, what if you knew the sphincter splitter was coming, so you pushed the "soft stool" button, to make the movement easier. No, there is a rhyme and reason for everything. There are times I swear my butthole must be open as wide as a mayonnaise jar, and it still hurts!

The other side to this dump, is that you have such great girth. I have taken dumps that resemble tuna cans, with such great width but no length. If I had my druthers, I'd just a soon take a normal dump as opposed to the sphincter splitter.

The diarrhea dump is the only dump in which you have no control. I cannot believe it sometimes when I turn around to admire my work and there is poop spattered everywhere inside the bowl. It's as if poop shoots out horizontally, once it hits the atmosphere. On occasion, I clean our toilets and I am always amazed when I see poop under the rim of the toilet. The poop doesn't hit the water, then shoot up does it? There is so much weird crap on the Internet these days, that I'm sure there is a toilet cam set up somewhere that would help me answer these questions. I can understand the diarrhea hitting the water and splashing a little residue within the bowl, but to actually creep all the way to the top of the bowl, confounds me. You know there is some power within, when you feel the cold toilet water splash up and rinse off your cheeks. Diarrhea is definitely the result of some dietary mishap. Drinking can result in a runny mess, but I am usually pretty consistent after a night of tipping a few. Sickness is a great excuse for having diarrhea, especially if you do it in your bed. Skid marks on the sheets, for example, can be caused by a small bout of the flu, but I feel it is either a wiping problem or you worked the mouse too long before you got up to take care of the problem. The diarrhea dump can also keep you on the toilet much longer than the normal dump. If you have it bad, you can finish, wipe and get up to go back to bed, to only be called back to the toilet before you get settled into bed. I've had diarrhea so bad that I've taken a pillow with me to the toilet, so I could rest my head on the wall while I waited for the next wave to hit. It was just a month ago that I got into something so bad, that I crawled up around the toilet with a pillow and a blanket and fell asleep, because I was so tired of getting up to go to the bathroom. There is the combo diarrhea/puke dump, in which you are doing both at the same time. There is a huge decision involved here and common sense usually wins out. What I'm referring to is what end you give the preference to, and what end you'd rather clean up off the floor. I have had times where poop was blasting out my butt, while barf was shooting out my mouth. We all know the worst case scenario, and I have been there. I was vacationing in Puerta Vallarta, when I must have eaten or drank something that didn't agree with me. I love Mexico and this is the only time I've ever gotten sick there, but that was a night I'll never forget. The first wave was nausea hit, so I headed to the bathroom to throw up. I assumed the position on my hands and knees when a surge came up my bowels and out my butt. It flew out with such a fury, it made it halfway across the bathroom floor. It was like I had a tidal wave gushing out my mouth while a volcano erupted out my butt. I had no choice, I had to keep my position and ride out the storm. It is bad enough having to dodge the barf splash, but in the back of my mind, I was already thinking about how fun it was going to be cleaning poop off the floor and walls of my bathroom; and this wasn't your normal, everyday smelling poop, it was dark, runny and had a stench that nearly made me cry. How about the ultimate in degradation, when you get up from the toilet after taking a dump, and before you have a chance to flush, you have to puke. This is real nice one because you have to turn your head the minute you let out the barf, to avoid getting slashed in the face with your own poop. I've been there and done that, but I hope it never happens again. I did not intend on bringing barf into the equation, but it does come into play with diarrhea at times. There is also the rainbow dump, which is associated with the diarrhea dump. The rainbow refers to the rainbow at the end of a storm. I liken this to the two part dump, in which the first part is runny, but finishes with a semi solid half. This signals the end of the storm and that happier times are on their way.

Hershey squirts fall somewhere between diarrhea and the hard pooplet. These little bastards are small, semi soft, wet and messy. These are huge contributors to skid marks and they also use up a lot of toilet paper. They always seem to find their way around your butt. I mentioned earlier how poop can spread every where; well these are the major culprits. This stool, (I love the term stool), is very wet and wild. It creeps out before you know what hits you. I'm sure the Hershey Corporation doesn't like this term, but it really does resemble semi, melted chocolate. It's like you eat a candy bar and before it can melt away, it heads south, greases the palm of the bouncer at *Club Sphincter,* and gets right in. I don't have this type of dump very often and I don't condone this type of behavior either.

I've touched upon a few of the many types of bowel movements and some of their characteristics, but I haven't brought up color. I read once in G. Q., that the darker the bowel movement, the better. It has something to do with how the colon does it's thing combined with the flow of blood in your system, or something along those lines. Let me get this misconception out of the way right now, I don't, nor have I ever subscribed to G. Q. I am a normal Joe who could give a shit less about fashion or colognes; I just received a complimentary copy in my mailbox one day and I read it. Anyway, back to color. Ever since I read that article, I always check out the color of my dumps. So far, I haven't been able to decipher whether my bowel movement is good, bad or ugly by it's color. There are different colors and I touched upon this subject in the first chapter. I give more to the size, consistency and shape, than I do color, but it is still an element of the bowel movement. I do think there is something to that article, because I feel the lighter brown or sometimes yellower the dump; the looser and smellier it is, whereas the darker dump has less of an offensive odor with a more solid consistency. I have nothing to base these assumptions other than a crazy article, but I feel pretty good about it. I won't go anywhere concerning the black dump. This is an ugly, scary dump and best to be avoided at all costs.

I have five dogs and they each take an average of two dumps a day, so in a week's time, I'm looking at picking up close to 70 dog dumps. If you don't think I have a little knowledge of bowel movement chemistry, you're crazier than I am. I just did my weekly pickup, and there was a huge number of black dumps, and this rose my curiosity. The dog's digestive system can't be that different than ours. I see some very human-like dumps out there in the grass, and it makes me proud. In fact, my dogs produce some very enviable bowel movements, but they, like us, have their different colors shapes and consistencies. They also have their good and bad dumping days. I sometimes catch one of the dogs in the act and I, being a curious animal, watch. I'd say ninety five percent of the time, their dumps are perfect. Two to four logs, solid but not too hard, light to medium brown with an acceptable range of smell. We like to believe that dog dumps

smell worse than our own, but I beg to differ. Different is not worse or better, it's
different. Let's not be ethnocentric here, we can't say their dumps smell worse
than ours, they just smell different. Of course there are those that smell so
different, that my nose hairs burn, but I don't hold that against them. Can you
imagine having to eat the same meal twice a day, every day? How much variation
can there be with their bowel movements? Plenty, believe me. Besides seeing
mostly perfect dumps lying about the yard, I also run into a few outlaw dumps.
There are the runny yellow, runny black, combination and the dumps with grass or
other nasties sticking out. If I mow my lawn and leave a pile of grass clippings,
the dogs will eat it like candy and produce these pure black, evil, monster poops.
They also have their Ex-Lax days, when they struggle to get anything out. It must
be embarrassing trying to take a dump as a dog, and be constipated. I watch these
poor animals and I have to feel sorry for them as they move around the yard,
trying to pinch out a small poop. If they are constipated or trying to pinch out a
pooplet, they will keep their butts crouched to the ground and walk around the
yard with their front legs. Elaine will tell me to quit looking at them, but I do
anyway. I'm sure my dogs don't embarrass easily, much like myself, but I can't
help but feel sorry for them. I have a dog now who likes to dump in the rocks. I
walk around my entire yard with my maximum size pooper scooper and try to

pick up every dump, because I feel you should be able to walk barefoot on a lawn without worry. I see different tendencies every week as to where the popular dump areas are. The rocks are a new one on me., but it is an easy dump to pick up, unless runny. There are hot spots and cold spots each week. One week, the area by the garage is empty and the next is like a dogshit convention. Maybe my dogs take a dump and go back to one of the other and say, " The big patch by the dryer vent is hot today", or "Stay away from under the tree, you'll get wet." We live in the Pacific Northwest so there are many rainy days, which still doesn't deter me from picking up the dog poop. I may be the only crazy person who picks up mushy piles of dog crap in the middle of winter up here, but I do it as a courtesy to my dogs. They don't like it when they have to sidestep poops in the yard. They look at me like I'm a slacker. I'll admit, I do let the dumps pile up at times during the real rainy season, but I look forward to the first freeze, because the dog dumps are frozen and easy to scoop up. I call them poopsickles. My dogs are spoiled, three of them sleep in our bed every night and the other two newcomers either sleep at our feet on the floor or out on the couches in the living room. On rainy days, they don't stray too far from the covered back deck, to take their poops. I watch as they saunter out onto the deck, and they actually look up into the sky before they walk into the yard. They will then walk out about six to ten feet, squat and do their business, then run back inside. It's pretty comical to watch. Picking up their dumps are actually easier in the winter because they are concentrated into a small area, whereas in the summer, they use every available inch of yard, because they can take their time in finding the perfect spot. I sometimes wonder if dogs aren't the superior species. How would we feel if someone fed us every day, let us sleep on beds and couches all day and then picked up our crap after we laid it anywhere we wanted. It really is a dog's life.

I have been pondering the perfect dump for some time now and to be honest, I can't come up the perfect bowel movement. The perfect dump is in the eye of the beholder, much like art, and taking a dump is an art project. I will describe my perfect dump and will then look forward to your card and e-Mails regarding yours. I am already starting on a sequel book. My perfect bowel movement is taken at home. Don't get me wrong, I have taken some stellar dumps on the road, but for the sake of argument, I feel my perfect dump is taken within the friendly confines of home. The toilet paper roll has to nearly full and the quality of tissue has to be both soft and thick. This will prevent any smearage when wiping. I like the lighting dim, but not dark, enough to read if I want. I have to be in comfy clothes, preferable sweats, shorts or something with elastic. I don't like a lot of noise, like running shower water or a dryer tumbling clothes. I like a quiet bathroom. I start working my perfect bowel movement when I wake up, so the morning is the best time for me. I get up and spend some time on the computer while I work the mouse, but I don't let the mouse out too far. When the time comes, I walk calmly into my spacious bathroom, pull down my comfy pants and sit on a cool toilet seat, not warm. If the seat is cold, that's okay too, I can make it work by giving it a few seconds to warm up. I then consummate the perfect bowel movement by giving it a little heave ho from within, a push of sorts, but not too much. My perfect dump doesn't need a lot of grunting, pushing or groaning, just a little nudge to get the logs rolling. I then feel the sphincter start to widen, enough to let me know the girth of the movement will be impressive, but not painful. My logs then start rolling out like an assembly line, one after another. There is no toilet water splashing in my perfect scenario, I prefer my sweet cheeks dry when I go to wipe. I then feel a light pressure release from within my bowels as the turds thunder their way into the cool, deep pool of toilet water. The smell is moderate, enough to let me know what I ate the day before, but not too pungent. My last log comes out perfectly tapered at the end and I then know a wipe isn't necessary, but I do it anyway. I roll a wad of toilet paper into my right hand, lift my right cheek and wipe from behind. One wipe does it all. I look at the toilet paper before I let it plunge to it's death, and I see very little to no poop, but my butt hole feels as clean as a spring day after a rain. I then pull up my stretchy pants, get up and admire my work. Four large logs and one smaller, tapered at the end. In total, the size of a foot long submarine sandwich. I give it a good admire, salute and then flush. The water swirls and with it, my perfect bowel movement goes down the pipes with nothing left behind, not even a toilet bowl skid mark.

One man's perfect dump is another's nightmare. Bowel movements are subjective, each with their pros and cons, but we all have to realize that we are living in a civilized society n which we shouldn't be judgmental. My observations are open for debate and I welcome an open, honest forum in which we can all open up and share our views, be it perverse, illogical or just plain wrong. We can make the world a better place to live if we share our common experiences and have a good laugh.

Chapter Eight

Odor Or Aroma, It's All In The Eye Of The Beholder

Do bowel movements have an odor or aroma? I guess it depends on you and your specific situation. I can honestly say that I have taken a few dumps in my day that smelled pretty good. In fact, my dad Larry used to say, "My bigs don't smell bad, they smell like fresh strawberry ice cream." I have to take a minute to explain the term "big". I think every family in the world has their own word for taking a poop, crap, shit, dump, number two, etc., and I'm sure many families use the normal vernacular for bowel movement. My family didn't use any normal verbiage to describe our poops. We were raised saying, going poop was "going big." Now where or how this ever came about is still a deep mystery to me. I can still remember playing on the school yard with my friends when a sudden bowel movement crept up on me and I'd say, "I'll be back in a minute, I have to go big."

You should have seen the looks on their faces when they heard me say that. Their

looks soon turned to pure, roaring laughter and they proceeded to give me all

kinds of hell about "Big." When I look back, I now realize that I was unable to

experience a normal childhood because I couldn't talk normally about my dumps

with my friends. Do you think I have just figured out why I'm writing this

perverted book? If I was seeing a psychiatrist, he would tell me that this was a

breakthrough for me. I'll let you in on another dirty little Gray family secret; we

called farts, "Poots." Yes, poots, and I'll be damned if I didn't meet the perfect

girl, (my wife Elaine), whose family also used this same expression for farts.

What are the odds of that happening? What a funny word, poot. I actually

remember hearing the word, poot, in a movie several years ago. It was in "North

Dallas Forty", the football movie with Mac Davis and Nick Nolte. In one scene,

Mac Davis, who I believe was portraying Dandy Don Meredith, says to Nolte,

"Aw, leave it alone Poot, we'll make it work", or something like that. Anyway,

that was huge for me, it told me there are others out there like myself, who also

used that word. Another breakthrough, maybe I should be writing a self help

book. I like the smell of strawberry ice cream, but I'll tell you, my dad's dumps

never smelled like fresh strawberry ice cream, let's get that on the record right now. There are various factors that make up the smell factor of bowel

movements. There is the strength, the length of the stench, the no smell, the food

you ate the day before, the match light, Glade Spray and many others.

I don't know why, but I have never smelled another person's poop that I didn't

think was rotten, foul and putrid. We have all walked in behind another person at

our office or at a sporting event after they have taken a dump. Why are other

people's bowel movements so offensive? I mean we are all human, we eat

basically the same foods day in and day out, so why does the food smell so much

worse coming out of someone else's butt, rather than our own? It could be that I

am dump prejudiced, or I'm a bowel movement bigot and that I stereotype stools.

The answer must lie within, within our different systems and bodies. I mentioned

earlier that the men's room in our office is exceptionally close to the center of the

main room. We have a can of Glade Air Freshener at close hand to the toilet and I

think it is gardenia scented. I would rather smell the onslaught of one's gnarly

dump, let it dissipate and get on with my day, than to walk by and smell gardenia

flavored poop. It's like the analogy of making a drunk, drink coffee, it only

makes him a wide awake drunk, which is twice as bad. Believe me, I bartended

for ten years. The aerosol laced dump is twice as bad as the real thing. I feel that

you should stand up and be a man after you take a dump in a public place. If you can't handle the heat, get out of the kitchen. I take responsibility for my actions and if I leave a big, gnarly dump smell in the bathroom, I walk out with my head held high.

There are those bowel movements that don't smell. How or why, I can't tell you. It's like the smell factory located in your sphincter was shut down for lunch when the batch of poop slid through for it's scenting. This also raises another interesting question, what comes first, the color or the smell? I mentioned earlier that there must be some type of inkjet factory located in the poop canal, that adds color to your dumps. There must also be an odor factory located in there also, so what comes first, the color or the smell? I look at it like this, the poop is first manufactured in the stool factory, it then arrives in the coloring plant. The size and shape definitely influence the color. After being colored, the dump is then shipped to the odor plant. This factory puts the finishing touches on the bowel movement, right before it emerges into the public spotlight. So there has to be times when the odor plant worker's are out having a smoke or an extended break, when one of these colored dumps arrives without being checked in. The dump waits awhile, then says, "Screw it, I'm going without any smell", and out it goes. I feel good about the no smell dump, and in fact many may argue that it is an element of the perfect dump, but I disagree. There has to be smell to be a perfect dump. In another effort to conceal the odor of a good bowel movement, some resort to using matches. My wife passed along some info the other day about her grandparents. As a little kid, she would go visit her grandparents in Fresno, California. She told me they kept a book a matches on top of their toilets. It isn't subtle, but I suppose it worked for them. I should probably try it, I like the smell of sulfur.

The time it takes for a dump smell to dissipate intrigues me. It obviously has something to do with the food I ate the day before, but why such a fluctuation in clear air times? My wife seems to think that when I fart in our bathroom, (which I do on occasion because I am a kind and thoughtful man), that the smell follows me back into our bedroom. Does dump odor do the same thing? I can take a dump with average odor and it can be gone within one or two minutes, but there are times when the odor clings to the walls and just won't go away. I think about the mad dumper at our office. He can take a dump at nine o'clock in the morning and I'll walk by at eleven, and still be able to tell you what he ate for lunch! It's like concentrate. His dumps must come in the concentrated form like orange juice, with more bang for the buck. There is no way he can like the smell of his own bowel movement.

Liking the smell of your own dump is a small pleasure in this ever complex world. It is a love/hate relationship. I love it when I take a gnarly dump with above average odor and I actually like the smell, but I hate it when the smell grosses me out. I had tacos a few nights ago and the next morning, I had to look down into the toilet to make sure there weren't tiny tacos floating around. The smell was bittersweet, it brought back the smell of taco meat simmering in my kitchen, but also burnt some of my nose hairs. I think we all take our bowel movements for granted. When was the last time you said to yourself, " that dump smells great"? I vow to start appreciating my bowel movements more often. I will admit that my dumps aren't generally too smelly, but I do have my moments. Now, when my wife reads this, I'm sure she will beg to differ, but that is my point, I really don't pay attention to my everyday dumps anymore. If you have kids and one is a problem child and the other is an ideal kid, you know you spend more time worrying about the problem child than the good one. It is the same with bowel movements, we fret and worry over our eye burning, paint peeling bowel movements, while we don't give our everyday, normal smelling dump a second thought.   Let's not get into this horrible mind set, let's revel in our everyday dump and appreciate him more.

I know my bowel movement smells bad when I can't stand the smell of it. My nose knows, and I feel sorry for anyone nearby, when I emerge from the bathroom. This same theory applies to farts, which by the way, have many similar characteristics as bowel movements. My farts tell me what is coming, sounding the alarm for the storm about to hit the shore, a dump so putrid that I ought to break out my goggles. A friend once commented to me that he thought it was amazing how, that when you know a dump is working it's way out the poop shoot, that a fart will squeak through and escape. I would think that it would be a hard line to break through, but they do. I cheated my way through chemistry, so I cannot get into a dissertation regarding the principles of gaseous versus solid materials, sorry. Let's just say I am a good judge of character and I know when a gnarly dump is coming. I attempt to keep my smelly bowel movements to myself, in my home surroundings because I am a courteous person, but when it comes on in a public place, I don't run and hide. Now my wife Elaine and Amber will hold their dumps for days if they knew a smelly one was coming, and they were stuck in a public place. I am reminded of a Seinfeld episode in which George Costanza holds his pee for days, while visiting India. I have lived this, I know this scenario with Elaine and Amber. I try to explain to them that this is a normal, bodily function that everyone in the world does, but my words go unheeded. The saddest part to this story is that most of the time, when I inquire about their dump later on in the day, they will shrug their shoulders and say, " I don't have to go anymore." Losing a bowel movement is a sin and a sad thing. Anyway, I always have mixed feelings when my dump is very smelly. On one hand, I am proud of the smell and how strong it is, but on the other, I worry about my insides and how they are taking the abuse. I may seem a bit callous, but I really do care about my system. I do enjoy my bowel movements, but when they cause me concern, things turn serious. I take my bowel movements seriously and I think everyone should. A job worth doing is a job worth doing well. I heard someone say once that taking a bowel movement was a waste of time, a laborious chore that was almost like being led to the gallows. I can get into the dynamics and psychological ramifications of this type of thinking, but I prefer to stay focused on the positive. I'm sure there are many people out there with pooping problems that would love to be able to get up and walk into their bathrooms everyday and take a normal bowel movement. It is their stories we should be telling here. My final words on this topic is that you don't know what you've got, until it's gone, so appreciate, respect and admire your bowel movements, and if you can, find a friend to share them with.

My dogs dumps are much like my own. They are consistent on a daily basis with good size, shape and smell. The smell of their dumps is not a good odor, but I am used to it, much like my own. They must like it, they are constantly smelling each other's buttholes. I wonder if prehistoric man or woman went around smelling each other's buttholes? I bet they did. I guess you would have to find fossils of a nose stuck in another man's anus, to be sure. This would also be the origination of the modern day term, "Brown Nose". I bet there were some pretty gnarly dumps back in prehistoric days. Imagine the smell of a bowel movement after feasting on Woolly Mammoth for three days. I can make many comparisons between my dog's dumps with mine, but the dog dump, after eating cat shit is where I draw the line. Yes, my dogs occasionally dig up a fresh pile of cat poop and chew on it like a Baby Ruth candy bar. Of all the dog dumps, this is one of the worst smelling. I don't make a habit of following my dogs around the yard smelling their bowel movements, but there are times when they go right in front of me, and I can't avoid smelling their freshly laid dumps. For some perverse reason, they like to follow me around the yard as I pick up their dumps with my fancy pooper scooper. Our cat does the same thing. I think they are proud of their accomplishments, which is more than I can say for many of us humans. This is another case of dogs being superior to human being, except for the smelling of buttholes and eating of catshit thing. On cold mornings, I sometimes catch a glimpse of one of them squatting, taking a great bowel movement and watch, as the steam rises off their freshly laid prize. This reminds me of a quick story. A fiend of mine, also named Kelly, and I used to have a running joke in high school. He commented to me one morning when he came over to pick me up, about the dog poop in our front yard, and I told him it wasn't dog poop, it was my mother's. I told him that if you got up early enough in the morning, you could catch my mother squatting in our front yard, taking her morning dump. He asked the reason why and I told him that she loved to watch the steam rise off her dump on cold mornings. Every time he came over to the house for the next five years, he's look down over the front yard and say, " looks like Pat has been out here again."

Bowel movements smell, and that is a fact, but there are some sweet smelling dumps out there. We just have to sift through the bad one's to really appreciate the good one's, and that is a lot like life.

Chapter Nine

Turn Around And Admire Your Work

We are all human, we all need positive reinforcement once in awhile. Turning around to admire our bowel movement is one of the most simple and gratifying of the reinforcements. I can't imagine those of you who get up after taking a great bowel movement and not turn around to admire your work. I realize there are many people who feel that poop is nothing to admire, but I feel different. It really is a shame to let such a good event pass through our lives without reveling in it, calling a friend or loved one into the bathroom to share it, or even just a phone call to a special friend to brag about it. My point is, let's bring our bowel movements out in the open and share a part of our lives that we have been taught to hide. Maybe parents can find a common ground between themselves and their troubled teens. Maybe world leaders should spend a few minutes with their counterparts detailing their latest dump. Can you imagine how different the Cuban missile crisis would have been if Kennedy picked up the phone, dialed Castro and said, "Fidel, John here, Coma Esta? I'm doing great, you should have seen the unbelievable dump I took this morning, it was the size of a submarine, which reminds me, what is this crisis everyone is talking about anyway, are we getting too uptight about this situation?". Don't you think that would bring a little bit of needed levity to the table? When you think about it, everyone in the world has three things in common; we all breathe air, eat food in some form and we all take dumps. We all need to take a little time to stop and smell the roses.

I, for one, do not get enough satisfaction or appreciation from many of my life's endeavors. My wife and I sell real estate for a living, after spending forty combined years in the restaurant business, (but that's another book). We do a damn good job of selling homes and we're proud of that. We sell thirty to forty homes a year and it takes a lot of hard work many times to keep transactions together. I spend quite a few restless nights fretting over these jerk off clients of mine and for what? We bust our balls every day, seven days a week for our clients, and we might see a thank you letter come our way once out of every one hundred closings. What's my point? My point is that none of us receive that pat on the back, or a "job well done", enough times in our lives. Turning around after taking an enormous, solid, sweet smelling dump is one of life's simple pleasures. Turning around after taking a bowel movement is my way of admiring my work, giving myself a pat on the back, telling myself a "job well done", and getting me started in a positive light, toward a new day. This is the ultimate in self gratification. It makes me feel good to see that I can produce something so simple, yet compelling to look at, and even smell at times. So I reach out to you and say, "turn around once in awhile to admire your work and give yourself a hand, a rousing round of applause, and you'll start feeling more fulfilled in your life's endeavors." A bowel movement is like a piece of art. An artist works on a painting or a sculpture and I work on my dump every morning, in pursuit of the perfect bowel movement. The perfect dump often eludes me, but I always strive toward perfection. There is no difference between me and the artist. We both strive toward the goal of producing the perfect piece of art. I have much in common with the artist. The artist and I both try to create our masterpieces in a creative atmosphere, in comfortable surroundings. The artist's loft is filled with inspiration and the tools needed to create. There is no difference between the artists loft and my bathroom at home. I have my reading material, an ample supply of soft toilet paper and I can change the lighting to go with my mood. I, like the artist sometimes brood over my creation, wondering when the inspiration will come, but I know it will eventually, and I stick to it until it empowers me to create. I am a bowel movement artist and with the correct frame of mind, you can be too!

With many of life's accomplishments, there can be let downs. I have been let down so many times after creating what I thought to be something of worth and value, when in actuality, it turns out to be a dud. Bowel movements are no different. If you decide to turn around to admire your work, you better be prepared to take the good with the bad. I have mentioned this before, but the bowel movement can be a trickster. I am fifty six years old and my butt hole still fools me once in a awhile. I sit down, take what I think is a substantial dump, turn around to admire my work, and my joy suddenly turns to shock and dismay. All I see is a small to medium sized turd, floating there all alone. How can this be? I think this is my butt hole telling me to not take anything in this world for granted. On the other hand, the opposite can also occur. Have you ever taken a dump that you believe to be small and below average, then turn around to be amazed at what just slid out your sphincter? That is one of life's little curve balls, a little treat, a surprise to help you start the day with a slight edge over everyone else. That's what gets you through your morning commute with a smile instead of a grimace. I think the lubrication effect helps make this bowel movement happen. The poop is so lubricated that it just slides on through with no hassles, thus tricking you into believing that you just took a small movement, when in actuality, it turns out to be a monster, a dump for the ages, a dump to be shared with the whole world.

This brings me to another topic; sharing your bowel movements. My friend Mark Sorenson and I spoke not too long ago and he had mentioned a web site in which people could post their bowel movements for others to share. We may have something here, although it would be tame compared to some of these other sites out there. Log onto www.bigbookofbowelmovements.com for more details, ideas and story sharing. There are those of us who are lucky when it comes to sharing and reveling in our bowel movements. I understand that in many families, the bowel movement wasn't a topic to be discussed, but a topic to be hidden in the closet and ignored like a little seen, drunken uncle. I am one of the lucky ones, my family shared our dumps with each other. My poor mother, she not only had to deal with my dad going "big", in his torn up undies in the dark, but she also had three boys to contend with. She used to tell people that she gave up trying to fight us, so she decided to join us. I think she made the wise choice. Looking back, she must have seen some incredible sights sitting there in our toilet bowls, including one of my rubbers that wouldn't flush down the toilet. My brothers and I would leave behind many of our dumps, although I now subscribe to the flush always theory. My nephew Eamon, from Hawaii, came out to live in Washington a year ago and I was glad to hear of his fascination with the bowel movement. He told me of taking a prize winning dump, a dump for the books, a dump colored bright blue. He told me he was freaked out because he didn't have anyone at home to share it with, and that made him sad. He decided to skip the flush and leave it behind for his younger brother Liam to admire. This story has a happy ending, you see Liam came home from school and got to see his older brother's work of art, even though it had lost some of it's color, shape, size and texture. He could still tell that he had witnessed something incredible. Liam came to visit us the following summer, and he too mentioned the same story and that it may have had a life changing influence on him. I have two other nephews in southern California and they have a particular interest in this book as well as an idea for a monthly "Dump magazine", complete with a dump of the month fold out. My brother Mike and I came up with that idea. Watch out Hugh Hefner, I may become the next publishing tycoon, but I can't imagine the type of girls that would drape themselves around the arm of the publisher of "Dump Magazine". I am glad to see the tradition being passed along the Gray family lines.

I am one of the lucky ones, I can share my dumps with my wife, although she has caught on to me. During our first years of marriage, when I would call her into the bathroom, she would come in, no problem. She then caught on to me. I have to be almost hysterical now to get her in to admire my work, but I can still pull it off once in awhile. I feel sorry for those of you closet dumpers, those who cannot share your daily Herculean feats with your loved ones. This is a major reason for writing this book, as I mentioned in the Forward. Dumps are not bad things, they are things that every human being does. We share our daily experiences with friends, coworkers and family, why not add bowel movements to the list. I'd much rather hear about a foot long, L shaped dump, than how bad the traffic was getting to work. Why be ashamed of taking a bowel movement, it is just a bodily function like burping or breathing, just funnier.

There are always a few questions I have to ask myself after taking a bowel movement. One is, should I wipe before I get up to turn around and admire? This is a question of purity. I sometimes wait on the wipe because I know that I have to see the dump in it's entirety, uncensored with no toilet paper covering it up in any way. I then sit back down and complete my wipe. This can cause a messy wipe, but if I'm getting up to admire my work before wiping, I'm pretty sure it's a perfect dump, and a messy wipe wouldn't come into play. The other question is whether or not to leave it behind. As I mentioned earlier, I believe in flushing; it's what separates man from animal, but it seems men at every sporting event

I have attended, believes otherwise. Have you ever walked into a public toilet when it was flushed? I don't think I have. My question is, do they ever flush at home? Maybe they aren't allowed to leave behind treasures at home, so they fulfill their dreams at the ballparks. These are the sad, unlucky ones who have to go through life without sharing their bowel movements with their loved ones. I can see these men as they emerge from those toilets. There is no life in their eyes and no spring in their step.

Another question that occasionally arises, is where did my dump go? Have you ever gotten up after taking a satisfying bowel movement to look down and see nothing but toilet paper? What a huge disappointment. This brings up the topic of floating and non floating bowel movements. Once again, I think the food we eat has a lot to do with this phenomenon. I have a theory and I'm sure there is a physiological answer to this question, but I prefer to go it alone. I believe the floating dump is one of high fiber and low fat content. This dump comes from eating bran, cereal, salads, vegetables and also carbonated beverages. Think there is a still a little bit of carbonation in the poop after it hits the water, to help keep it afloat. This also applies to beer, which is always an important part of everyone's daily dietary intake. The sinking poop is a large, hulking, heaping mass. Due to the fact that my diet is somewhat varied, I split my time between the sinking and the floating bowel movements. I cannot, however tell you which is my favorite, that would be like having to tell someone which of your children you love the most. You love them equally, of course. I feel the same way with my dumps, they are individuals with unique qualities, and I admire and respect that.

There are two types of sinking dumps; there is the "sink/disappear dump" and there is the "sink/lie on the bottom of the bowl dump". We are all familiar with these types of sinking bowel movements. I feel the most common of the two is the "lie on the bottom" sinker. This dump is nothing special except that it can have tremendous volume. There is usually a rank smell associated with this poop, which is all right, as long as you're not crossing the line of unbearableness. The wipe on this one can be messy, with sometimes having to go in three or four times for a clean wipe. This is probably the most common bowel movement at this point in my life, and I feel good about that. The "sinking/disappearing" dump has it's good and bad qualities. The disappearing dump is usually streamlined and smooth, like a new shiny submarine, gliding through a moonlit bay. It must have enough lubrication to slip on through the anal cavity, splash into the cool toilet water and slip into the deep abyss without a trace. It is kind of a secret agent poop, not wanting anyone to know it's identity or whereabouts. I have to admire this dump for it's craftiness and stealth like capabilities. Another great trait this dump has, is the wipe. There is virtually no wipe involved here, and yet we see nothing when we whip around to admire, except a nearly perfect piece of ivory colored toilet paper, floating alone, wondering where the poop went.

The one and only negative aspect to the disappearing dump is the feeling of being violated, robbed and stripped of that proud feeling we otherwise get when we turn around and admire our bowel movements. It's like going to one of your kid's big soccer or football games, and they sit on the bench the whole game. This is a travesty, an injustice in this world I cannot control. We work hard to make a life for ourselves and our families, and yet there are those bowel movements that disappear on us, like a favorite child going bad and running away. We have to realize that our bowel movements are like our children, and we have to love them for their good and bad qualities. To sit on a toilet, work out a good, solid bowel movement and to not turn around to admire your work, well, that is wrong. Take a few minutes for yourself every day to stop and smell the roses or strawberry ice cream if you are my dad. We deserve to praise ourselves for a job well done. In this crazy world of drugs and teen violence, a few minutes spent admiring a great bowel movement is time well spent.

Chapter Ten

Stories You Wouldn't Tell Your Mother, Unless She Was Mine!

This chapter is a culmination of the previous chapters. I have had a ball writing this book and I hope I have gotten a chuckle or two out of you. The best part to writing this book, is being able to share it with people. I have friends that have been asking me "How the book's coming", and want to read what I've written so far. I recently sat next to a woman I greatly admire. She has been a teacher/principal for many years and just received her doctorate. She was asking me about things and the topic of hobbies came up. I said, "well, I am currently writing a book, and I hope to get it published". She then asked me about the book. I then replied, "Gloria, I don't know if you'd be interested in this topic". You see, Gloria is my bosses wife! She pried it out of me, and to my shock, she squealed with laughter and delight. This made me feel pretty good about my endeavor. I recently had a few friends over for a barbecue and a few beers, and the topic of my book came up. There were a few folks there that had no idea how perverted I was, but before long, we were all sharing our most embarrassing dump stories and laughing hysterically. This is why I wrote this book. This last chapter is for you out there, who isn't embarrassed to tell a humiliating story about a bowel movement mishap. I am also proud of the title to this chapter, because my mom died while I wrote this book, but that isn't sad, she loved to tell a great story and I know she is proud of me.

First Recollection

My first recollection of pooping my pants was sheer horror. I don't know how old I was, but I was walking and wearing shoes. I still remember I was wearing a pair of those little blue overalls. Overalls are great, I had a pair in high school I wore almost daily, but there is was one drawback, when a fast moving dump roars along, it is hell trying to get those overalls off in time. Anyway, I was out in my front yard playing around in the dirt with my matchbox cars, when the urge came on me like a fright train roaring down the tracks. I didn't have enough time to get in the house, I froze. I wore underpants then, but they did me no good. The poop must have snuck past the undie guards, because it came shooting down my leg like a hot lava flow. I was young and inexperienced at this sort of thing, so I freaked out. I think I cried for my mom, but she did not hear her little boy's cry for help. The most vivid recollection I have is the hot poop running down my leg. I stood there next to our huge olive tree in my front yard and just let it run down my right leg. I still think about what I did next, and I can't figure it out to this day. While the hot poop was running down my leg, I bent down, untied my right tennis shoe and pulled my foot out. Why? I don't know. As I stood there with my heel pulled out of my shoe, I felt the poop slide down my calf and land right in my shoe. It damned near filled the entire shoe! They were great shoes too, they were those black Converse tennis shoes. So there I was, standing in my front yard, with poop running down my right leg, soaking into my overalls and filling my right Converse tennis shoe. I had no choice, I put my shoe back on and walked into the house and yelled for my mom to come help. That was my first remembrance of a bowel movement debacle, but little did I know that I was only getting started, there were more to come.

A Walk Home From School

This story comes from my wife Elaine. Elaine was a cute little kid, you should see her pictures. She told me not to mention her name in this story, but I am anyway. She was a little kid, living in Oregon, maybe six or seven years old and she was walking home from a hard day of first grade. The sudden urge to poop all over the place hit her hard and hit her fast, she never had a chance. She was wearing a little pink dress and underpants. She started home in hopes of making it to sanctuary, but she was not fast enough. The running motion caused the poop to come out even quicker, and this was a little girl trying in vain to stop the inevitable. I have to give her some credit here, she didn't lie over and let it happen like I did in my first experience. I feel the tears well up as I write this horrible tale. The poop came on too fast to even think about an alternate plan, so she pooped her panties. She says it felt so huge and heavy in her underpants, that it was drooping down below her dress line. Now that is a healthy bowel movement! She ran as fast as she could with her little legs, but the poop drooped lower and lower In her underpants. It was a disaster. Her only hope was that there wouldn't be anyone home to witness this debacle, and her prayer was answered. She ran in the front door headed straight to the bathroom. She pulled her pants down and the poop was smeared all over the place. She claims she used an entire roll of toilet paper to cleanup the mess. Every time she wiped, she smeared it more. She was such a mess, she made the decision to ditch the underpants in hopes of covering up one of the greatest dump disasters of her young life. Kids are funny, when they get into a jam, they don't consider what would happen if they just told someone, no, the most important thought in their minds at that time, is how and where to stash the evidence, completely absolving themselves of the incident. Unfortunately, most adults are the same way. She scoured the house, looking for a place to dump the evidence. She was smart enough to realize that the trash can would get her busted, so she looked for a spot outside. She took and dumped her underpants in a vent on the outside of the house, near the crawl space. She reminds me there were no protective screens back then. This sounds like the happy ending to a tragic tale, but alas, it was not to be. Eight years later, when young Elaine was budding into a beautiful teenager, she was helping pack up the house for a move. Her mother, for some odd reason, decided to look under the house. Yes, the underpants were there in all their glory. I imagine they didn't smell anymore, but the fourteen year old Elaine was busted big time. Elaine has always told our daughter Amber, that if you ever try to hide anything, whether it's a lie or evidence of any kind, that you'll always get caught. I now know where this advice comes from. This tale teaches us all a lesson, don't dump your poopy undies under the house or you'll get caught brown handed.

Baby tales

I mentioned a good friend of mine earlier in the book named Jake Stub. He is a character and a true lover of bowel movements. He and his lovely wife Sandy recently had their second child and to that, I say congratulations. I haven't heard from Jake in a while, he must be busy trying cases, but he does like to share his baby's bowel movements with me. One of the last calls I received from Jake was about a year ago, and he was beaming with pride as he spoke to me on the phone. He was so excited about his oldest baby's dumps, that he put his wife on the phone to back up his story. She seemed pretty excited herself. He has a good woman there. Anyway, there he was on the phone describing to me, the size and girth of his baby's latest dump. From the description he gave, it must have been the size of a 24 ounce can of beer. It hurt my sphincter listening to his description. He said he was so proud of his child and that his dumps were sometimes overshadowed by his own baby's. He didn't go into the specifics of his new child's masterpiece, but he did mention the stench and not in a bad way, but in an almost proud, bragging fatherly way. I am glad for Jake and his family, I see a smooth road ahead for the Stub Clan.

Family Genes

This is a quick story about our daughter Amber. I married Elaine when Amber was about seven or eight years old, so I missed all the fun, baby poop action. Elaine told me a few stories about the baby Amber that made me laugh. It seems that the Amber was at the age from which she still ate from the highchair. My parents kept me in a highchair until I was about ten, and that probably explains some of my deep seeded problems. Back to the Amber. Elaine fed her some creamed corn, which turned out to be a huge mistake. Elaine claims that Amber had diarrhea for days, even weeks, although I find *weeks*, to be stretching the truth a bit. One day, Elaine is feeding the baby Amber in her highchair when this runny, stinky poop starts running out of her diapers and down her legs. Elaine couldn't get her to stop. She kept wiping her off, hoping she would quit, but to no avail. Now mind you, this is years before Elaine and I met, and many years before she knew my bowel movement philosophy, but she pulled a Kelly right there in her home. She took the little, poop stained baby Amber, highchair and all, into the shower and hosed her down like an animal in the zoo. She didn't even take her out of the highchair, there she was sitting under a stream of warm water flowing out from the shower head, still strapped into her highchair. Sounds like she is related to me!

Still in the family genes, come these recent poop stories from the Amber and her one year old baby. It seems Grandbaby Attle has some work to do with her digestive phase. A few weeks ago, our daughter fed the baby some baby food with chopped up carrots in it. A few hours later, Amber found the full pieces of carrots sitting in her diaper. I can do that with lettuce and corn, but not carrots, ouch! This following picture comes to us from Elaine latest visit to see the grand baby's first birthday. Elaine was gone a week and she called me from Texas to tell me about this dump. This is the diaper following a meal with spinach in it. I wonder if Popeye ever had it this bad.

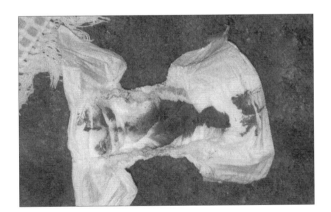

The last baby story, (I promise), has to do with the grandbaby, or Attle as we now affectionately call her. Amber says that Attle was happily soaking in the tub, playing with her toys, when these unidentified objects started floating to the surface; like those little frogmen you had as a kid, that you put those little pellets in, and watched dive and return to the surface. Well, these frogmen didn't dive, they just floated on top. Adalei seemed unaffected and undisturbed by this little mishap, she kept playing along with her toys happily. Ah, the joys and innocence of youth. I wonder what would happen if at our next party here at the house, I invited everyone into the hot tub, and pulled a stunt like the Adalei. It would be a scene right out of Caddyshack, which is still one of my favorite cult movies.

Pat

Pat is my mother, God rest her soul. She suffered a malady termed Irritable Bowel Syndrome. It hurts my butt just to think of it. I have inherited my hairline from Pat's side of the family, I hope I.B.S. isn't next. She was either constipated for days on end or she was shitting all over the place, but she took refuge in any normal bowel movement and loved to tell us about it. I felt bad for her most of the time, but she would come up with some great stories that made me laugh. Many of her poops were of the Milk Dud variety; small, hard and hard on the butt hole. She would call us or we would talk to her on a daily basis during the last months of her life, and the topic would always shift to bowel movements, and this I didn't mind. I like talking dumps, it seems that for an instant, you forget your everyday problems and worries, plus dumps are funny and we all like to laugh. Many of her bowel movements, as I mentioned, were small and hard, and she let me know. I'd say, "Did you take a dump today mother?", and she'd say, "Yes, shit, nothing but little pooplets." Her comment made me laugh and it shouldn't have, but it did anyway. My mother had a foul mouth so she would describe these pooplets as "little fuckers", or "little bastards", and that made me laugh even harder. We actually brought in strangers to one of our dump conversations once, and it was an intense deal, believe it or not. I went to the nursing home to visit Pat one morning, and that was my first mistake. You see, she had a morning routine in which she had to get up, take her medication, sit around, have a cup of tea and then start working on her dump. I applauded her for that, it's good to know your morning dump routine, and stick to it. Now the day I showed up, I walked in to Pat having a very heated discussion with two of her nurses about her morning bowel movement routine. At first, I was flabbergasted, but soon, I chimed in like a pro. It seemed the nurses needed to get her up at 6:00 a.m. on

Tuesdays, so she could go in and take a shower. Now I am a reasonable man, but

if anyone woke me up at 6:00 a.m. and rushed me into a shower, it would piss me

off, and it would definitely ruin my morning bowel movement. We were faced

with quite a dilemma and neither side was backing down. We had the classic

confrontation between the inflexible corporate rules and regulations versus the

little guy, just trying to take a dump in peace. I see Shirley McClain playing my

mom, Louis Fletcher reprising her role as nurse Ratchet (from One Flew over the

Cuckoos Nest), and Jack Nicholson playing myself, in a runaway, summer

blockbuster movie. By the way, some say I resemble jack, I just wish my bank

account resembled his. So, this discussion gets to the point of yelling between my

mother and the nurses. I have to step in with my charm and smooth ways to settle

this matter. I slowly rise up from my chair and say, "Fuck it!". They all stop and

stare at me in disbelief. I then proceed to tell them that the morning bowel

movement is the cornerstone to my mother's day, every day, and if this shower

routine can't resolved, then I will have to speak to the owner of the establishment

at once. I see Nicholson pulling off this scene with his usual, sarcastic perfection.

I told them that Irritable Bowel Syndrome doesn't just make her bowels irritable,

it also makes my mom irritable. Pat then gets a little teary and starts describing how her poops are every morning and that she needs a good, normal dump once in awhile. It was a sad moment, but I was laughing inside. To make a long story short, we did work out a new shower schedule and it did not conflict with Pat being able to complete her morning routine.

There are many other tales from my mother as you would have guessed, but I'll limit it down to just two. The first story actually reminds me of my wife's story of walking home from school, but with a little twist. Up until about a year ago, Pat was still driving her little, orange 1972 Camaro to the store to do her shopping. She was in her early seventies and she was wearing those Depends or Attends, whenever she went out. I don't blame her, I would like to wear them to Seattle Seahawk football games to save me from having to wait in those long bathroom lines. So, she is finishing her shopping at Safeway, when the mouse starts poking his nose out. When the mouse poked his nose out with Pat, it was a huge deal. She hurried out of the store, which might have been her problem. As you remember, Elaine hurried home from school and that prompted the mouse to come running out too. Pat thought she had it under control, as many of us have felt as well, but she was wrong. She loaded her groceries into her car, started it up and drove home, but the mouse was in control of this little joy ride. According to Pat, "the poop started running like pudding." She stepped on the gas to get home quicker, but not even the Depends would help her with this disaster. She pulled into her driveway and the entire car smelled like poop. At this point, she thought the Depends had done their job and contained the flood, but she was wrong again. She made it into the house, but not after leaving a trail of hot, mushy poop in the dirt from her driveway to her backdoor. She then made it to the bathroom where she proceeded to pull herself together enough to sit down on the pot. Most of the movement had already moved, so she had no choice but to pull a bathtub cleanup move. You must think that everyone in my life just heads straight into the shower or bathtub instead of wiping themselves. You might be right. With the use of the shower nozzle, she rinsed off the evidence. The funniest part of the story is how she dealt with the poop in the driveway. She asked her seventy five year old, next door neighbor man if he would wash it off for her, and he did! What are neighbors for?

The second tale is similar, but I actually got to witness the destruction this time. I called her in the morning to talk about nothing, when she started in on her IBS worries and that she hadn't gone poop in three or four days. I seem to surround myself with these women who hold their poop for days on end. Anyway, I asked her if she had taken anything for it and she replied that she had taken a huge amount of Metamucil. With all these name brands I'm throwing

Around, you'd think I could land an endorsement deal or two. I should have invested in Metamucil years ago, today I'd be a rich man with Pat's purchases alone. You see, she was either constipated or pooping all over the place; there were very few normal poop days for my mother. She would either be taking medicine for constipation or diarrhea, what a vicious circle. I told her I would be over a little later and hung up. I later walked into her house and there she was, sitting at her dining room table, just staring out the big picture window at all the huge pine trees. She seemed fine, without a care in the world, until I smelled something horrible. I asked her if everything was all right and she turned around in her chair and said, " I had an accident", and pointed down to the floor. Once again, here was the trail, but this was a trail of wet, pure liquid stains that smelled like Metamucil. The trail was in a neat row, starting from her chair and ending up in the bathroom. I could tell she was upset, so I didn't start laughing right away, but instead, acted like Sherlock Holmes and followed the trail to see if I could recreate the events of the crime scene. I saw where it started, in the dining room, and followed it onto the vinyl floor in the kitchen. She managed to clean up most of that mess, but the trail picked up again in her sitting room, where for a few feet, I lost track. I then looked up and to my horror, I found some poop stuck to the wall! How did a seventy two year old woman manage to shoot poop all over the

Wall? I was actually envious, what a great party trick. I looked at her and asked her how the poop got on the wall, and she responded by saying, " I didn't have my undies on, and when I crouched down like a hunchback and tried to run for the toilet, it must have shot out of my butt and hit the wall". I shook my head in disbelief and let out a small, but controlled laugh, I didn't want to make her feel like an idiot, but I wanted to bellow with laughter. My laugh was just what the doctor ordered, because Pat started laughing along with me. Even though I was laughing hysterically, I really did feel sorry for her. I picked up the trail again, until I finally made it into the bathroom where, once again, the walls had been hit hard. For an older woman, she must have had some huge pressure built up top let go of a blast like that. I admired her attempt at a cleanup, I would have done the same. The Mount St. Helen's blast must have paled in comparison to Pat's blast. Elaine has an expression for this type of dump, and she calls it a "blast from the past." When you think about it, it is right on, because you have the past build up of poop in your system and when it comes out, it blasts out. Very good, maybe this expression will become an American icon. To finish the story, I cleaned up the remaining debris while cracking jokes to relieve Pat's dismay. Elaine later had to take a steam cleaner to get the poop stains out of the carpet. Wow, see what a lot of us have to look forward to when we get older, what a life. I lost my mom in March and I owe much of my demented sense of humor to her.

I lost my mom in March and she was kept up to date on the writing of this book. She would give me this funny look and ask me how the book was coming along and I'd tell her about the latest chapter or story and she'd shake her head like a mother always does and smile. I think she would be proud.

Dog dumps

I have always been around dogs. As a kid, I still remember sitting in the garage as our English Springer Spaniel gave birth to nine puppies. It was corny, but my folks named them all after flowers, so we had a Petunia, Daisy, Rosie, Daffodil, Tulip and so on. Ever since that time in my life, I have always had at least two dogs in my life. I figure that for thirty years, with at least two dogs, at two dumps a day, that at the very minimum, I have seen and picked up at least 43,800 canine craps. That makes me somewhat of an expert I guess, so I'll continue. You have to realize that those figures are computed with a minimum of two dogs, I now have **five**!, and they aren't little yipper dogs, these are five big dogs; three Labradors and one Doberman and a Husky mix. It is a long story, but to sum it up quick, we took on Pat's two Labradors when she passed, bringing our total up to five. We would have six if we hadn't suddenly lost one of our yellow Labs to a back problem two years ago. I feel a little sorry for the new dogs because there has to be some sort of crapping criteria for dogs, you know, where the hot spots are and where the off limit areas are located. I think they are adjusting well, but I still see some major faux pas out there in the yard. For example, there is a well worn trail that runs through our backyard that our dogs have made in their daily sojourns. Until the new dogs, Chrissy and Paddy came along, there was never a dump left in this trail, it was off limits, because dogs are smarter than we give them credit for, they do not like stepping in their own poop. I sometimes watch them on cold rainy mornings as they look up into the sky and seem to tiptoe around the yard until they find a suitable spot to take a bowel movement. My dogs are spoiled and I will admit that to anyone, but I still laugh when they walk on the wet grass like they were walking through a pit of burning coals. The trail thing isn't the only change I've noticed. We live on a half an acre which is fully landscaped with lawn, trees, shrubs and gravel walkways. The gravel walkways were always left clean and pure by my hounds for some peculiar reason. Like I said, they are smarter than we think. The sanctity of the walkways have been recently breached, I find dog poop all over them and I don't know what to do. I can't teach old dogs new tricks and I don't feel like spanking the dogs for dumping on rocks, I guess I'll learn to live with it.

There has only been one year that I haven't had dogs and that was in 1988, the first year Elaine and I were married. We were doing the move from one condo to another thing, and it was hard to find a place that allowed pets. We finally settled in and moved into my Grandfather's home in Laguna Hills, California. He was living in a convalescent home and the family wanted to rent it out, so we obliged. We immediately got word of a litter of Labrador / Retriever pups. We snatched up two, and still kick ourselves for not taking three. We named them Sunshine Lee and Hana Marie. These two were hell on wheels together for many years, before they mellowed out. My dad used to come over to stir them up and watch them tear around the yard and house like wild Banshees. I have many dog dump stories, as you can imagine, but I'll try to pin it down to a few of my favorites.

Hana and Shiner were almost identical twins and they were as cute as could be, but there were a few traits that set them apart. For one, Hana loved chocolate and had a huge sweet tooth. As I write this, Elaine came in to tell me that Hana has been eating all our blueberries and strawberries! Anyway, I think I know where she developed this taste. When Hana and Shiner were about two years old, we had a friend watch them for us at our house, while we vacationed in Europe for three weeks. (I don't think our friend was ever the same again). It was Christmas time, so we came home with lots of goodies, wrapped them and put them under the tree. Elaine and I seemed to notice an absence of presents from

Under the tree. We both got on our hands and knees, looked under the tree, and we were right. We couldn't figure out what would have happened to the wrapped presents, so we started to look around. After searching the house, we move our search to the backyard. Hana and Shiner had a little stash in the backyard, full of unwrapped Christmas presents. We were so pissed off, thankfully we laugh about it now, but these were to our family from Germany and Switzerland. We figured out what happened. The dogs must have smelled Swiss chocolate in one of the presents, grabbed it and took it outside to enjoy. (To this day, Hana still unwraps presents, and she is eleven years old.). Our theory is that once they got into the great package full of Swiss chocolate, they figured that every other present under the tree was also full of chocolate. There must have been fifteen, unwrapped presents sitting out there in their little cache. The amazing thing is that all the wrapping paper was all kept in a little bundle, so as not to raise suspicion when we looked out in the yard. I realize this isn't a bowel movement story, but I had to set the scene for the next two stories.

Hana and the Chocolate Bars

Our daughter, Amber must have been about ten or eleven years old when she came home from school one day with a box full of chocolate candy bars to be sold for some school project. They were quite good actually, and Hana agreed. Elaine, Amber and I went out for dinner one night and left the dogs in the house. Like I said, our dogs are spoiled. The Amber made a fatal mistake that dark and stormy evening, she didn't hide her chocolate bars from the dogs. Hana didn't look too good when we got home. Shiner had locked herself in one of our bathrooms, so she was off the hook. The dogs used to get themselves locked in rooms when the doors would close behind them, and they still do it once in awhile. We even have those child proof hasps installed on our pantry door and the under the sink-trash drawer, but Hana and Shiner figured out how to open those within two weeks. Anyway, Shiner is in the bathroom whining and Hana is just standing there with these huge, dilated pupils, wagging her tail. We couldn't figure it out until the Amber went in to check her candy bar stash. She was a very good bookkeeper, so she knew what she had in stock always, partially because of my sweet tooth. The Amber comes racing out of her bedroom in tears, and says, " there are fourteen candy bars missing!:. Hana sensed our displeasure and tried to slink out into the darkness of the night, but we caught her. She actually had some of the foil wrapping stuck in one of her teeth. She was busted big time. We couldn't believe it, we were all in a state of shock; fourteen candy bars? She had emptied the remainder of the box, and was probably looking for more. Hana was panting like a wild animal with dilated eyes, and as my parents used to say about every teenager, she was acting like she was " hopped up on goof balls!". We didn't know what to do, so we let her run it off in the backyard. I do have to say the dumps were huge, plentiful and smelled pretty good. This is a story I frequently tell at parties, but I add another ending to the story for effect. The ending I love to throw in for laughs, is that when Hana started her chocolate bar dumps, they were all individually wrapped in foil and wrappers, and that the dump's were in such condition, that we gave them back to the Amber, to sell to our favorite neighbors.

Cookie baking day

Every year Elaine and I host an annual Christmas cookie baking day. The object is to bake as many cookies, fudge and goodies as possible before we get too drunk to clean it up. No, really, we do hand out nice platters of cookies to offices, nursing homes and neighbors. We don't have a huge kitchen, so we all pile in with our recipes and start rolling, sifting, measuring, eating and drinking. I usually play bartender, but I have since started contributing a batch or two of Toll House cookies. The kitchen gets very crowded and not only with people, but with dogs also, they are very much a part of the action. They get everything that falls on the floor and they take advantage of it. In 1997 we had three dogs; Sunshine,

Hana and Dobie Wan Kenobi and they were always underfoot. We would yell, but they would keep coming back for more. After a few hours when the liquor started taking effect, the dogs were no longer a nuisance, they had become a part of the experience. I would look over at Bob, with a cocktail in hand, slipping Shiner a piece of fudge, or Crystal sliding a cookie to Hana, but at that point, we didn't care. As the day wore into evening, we were close to finished, and we were pleasantly buzzed as well. We always put all of our creations on top of the hot tub, so the dogs won't get into them, and it worked, but we forgot to put everything away in the kitchen. Mistakes are capitalized on very often around here, and we made one. We were in bed when Shiner comes running into our bedroom, jumps up on the bed panting like a hyena. She was soaking wet, and I mean soaking! There were drops of water falling off her fur, onto our sheets. We ran into the kitchen and found nothing on the counter, where a full brick of baker's chocolate had been sitting. Shiner had eaten a full pound of pure, unsweetened chocolate. Shiner then raced by us to get outside. I followed her, but lost her in the darkness. It was pouring outside, cold, miserable and very dark. I could hear Shiner Dog doing something, but I couldn't see her. We got out a flood light and caught her as she darted between all our border trees. We have those trees that grow tall and right next to each other, so Shiner was weaving her way in and out of the trees. She then scampered out into the grass, squatted and shot out a true Hershey squirt. I had to examine this more closely, so I wandered out into the yard, as Shiner dog took to the trees again. The poop was steaming and pure black. I quickly wondered about the effects of white chocolate. I turned my gaze back upon Shiner's Toll House poopies. I shined the flashlight around the grass and the steaming, chocolate dumps were everywhere. It looked like those pictures you see of the geysers in Yellowstone park, with all the steam rising. The poor dog had eaten a pound of chocolate, gotten so hot that she had to cool herself off by running in the rain, through all our trees and occasionally stopping to squirt out a burning hot, mushy black poop. I don't think I have ever felt so sorry for an animal. She was miserable; running around., soaking wet, all hopped up and shitting her brains out. We actually called our Vet at home and he told us she'd be all right, but I think she learned her lesson. You'd think that Hana would have warned her about such things. I woke up the next morning and looked out into the backyard, and between the dark piles strewn through the grass ands the trees being knocked about, it looked more like Omaha Beach after the D-Day landing.

Boot Camp

My dad Larry was a character. He bore a striking resemblance to Carroll O'Conner, the actor and Jack Nicklaus, the golfer. He was a rotund man and in fact, I remember one time when he returned from seeing the doctor about his weight. Larry said to us, " the doctor says my weight is fine….. For a man eight foot tall." That was about right, but we all loved big Larry. He was fun, jovial, liked his cocktails and loved to tell a good story.

He told me a tale years ago that still makes me laugh. He served in World War Two, in the Pacific with the Navy. He signed up like most other red blooded Americans during that time. He started his illustrious military career, as everyone did, in boot camp. Larry was not very good at taking orders, so I can imagine how he fared in the Navy. It seems my dad did not get along very well with his drill instructor during boot camp. According to Larry, he was always picking on him, and I can't imagine why. Anyway, one day during his boot camp regime, they blew revele at 5:30 a.m., so Larry hurried on his clean, pressed uniform and reported out in front of the barracks, where they all lined up at attention. My dad was about to begin one of the worst days of his life. It seems the mouse started poking his nose out, then and there during the morning roll call. Larry told me how horrible the food was in the Mess, so I can picture some gnarly dumps. The mouse wasn't going to wait for anybody, he came out at roll call also. My 'Ol man raised his hand to speak to the Drill Instructor. The D.I. came over and asked my dad what his problem was, and Larry told him. According to Larry, the Drill

Instructor got a big grin on his face and told him he was not excused and that he

was not allowed to hold up the entire squad because he had to take a dump. Larry

held it for as long as he could, he was a brave soldier; but he would lose this

battle. The day that lay ahead for my dad was not ideal for his situation. The first

of the activities was calisthenics, followed by a three mile run and finished with a

trip through the obstacle course. Larry didn't even make it through the exercises

before he let the first of his dump slide into his shorts. What a nightmare, he had

just started your day and his undies are already full of shit. The three mile run

was a long one with his shorts full of hot, runny poop. He felt poop slide down

his leg about one and a half miles into the run. He was miserable, his butt started

to chafe and he started to stink pretty bad. His comrades knew what was going

on, so they stayed as far from him as possible. He figured that if he finished the

run, that the D.I. Would let him take a trip to the can. He was wrong. There was

no break, no letup and no time between the time finishing the run and starting the

obstacle course. Larry said it was the worst day of his life, and I believe that. He

had to crawl under webbed rope, climb across jungle bars, climb a rope and climb

a wall near the end of the exercise. In the meantime, his under shorts are still full

of hot, stinky, filthy poop, with more slipping down his leg with every step.

Larry said he didn't have a problem with under the rope, but on the jungle bars, he felt more poop run out of his shorts and down his leg. He also said nobody was talking to him at this point in the day. He tried to climb the rope, but only made it halfway. I'm sure the wetness of his crotch didn't help him with the grip needed to climb a rope. I feel sorry for the next guy on the rope, imagine what he was gripping and smelling. Larry also said he just lost it when he had to run from one section to the next and when he saw the wall, he didn't care anymore. He had shit in his pants for over two hours and half of it had run down his leg, and now he was supposed to run, leap and climb over a wall. I am not a military man and I don't know what the consequences are regarding going AWOL, but I would have given it my best shot at this point.

Larry barely made it over the wall and the Drill Instructor was in his face the entire morning. He yelled, he screamed at Larry, and even told him he smelled like shit, which was definitely true, but Larry kept his cool under pressure and finished the course. They were all excused for breakfast at this point, but Larry didn't eat. He was ordered to drop his pants in front of the barracks while another recruit took a hose to his lower half, while many of the recruits stood and bellowed with laughter. This may be one of the most heroic tales that came out of World War Two. Whenever I'm having a bad day, I think back to this story, and it somehow makes my day seem like a walk in the park.

The Coffee Can

This story comes to you from the beautiful Sonoma Valley in California. A very good friend of mine, Tommy McDonald and I took a trip back in 1982, up the coast of California. I was attending San Diego State and he was going to U.C. Santa Barbara. We both worked our way through college by working in the restaurant business. We both ended up staying in the business nearly twenty years, but that's another story. My college was on a semester system, so classes didn't begin until late September every year. I took this opportunity to drive my 1968 V.W. van up the California coast every year. I'd spend two to three weeks exploring the coastline and deserted valleys. It was great, everyone should do it.

I called Tommy to see if he was interested in joining me, and he jumped on it. We were fully prepared for anything. We had coolers full of ice cold beer, groceries, spare gas, oil, my dog, our surfboards and of course, plenty of contraband. We made our way up the coast, through San Francisco and into wine country. We happened to meet a very nice gal who worked for Kenwood winery, who let us spend a few nights at her place. We left a few days later and headed up the highway, toward Humboldt, where I spent my first year in college.

We all inherit traits from our parents. I mentioned earlier that my unfortunate hairline comes from my mother's side of the family. Pop was as bald as a bat. My question is how we inherit habits or moods. I'm sure there is a geneticist out there who can explain it, but I can't figure it out. What I'm getting at, is that I inherited my father's driving habits. Once he got on the road, there was no stopping him. If he was hot, he rolled down all the windows full blast and didn't care if everyone was cold. He yelled at other drivers, calling them obscene names. He even flipped off a cop once, and the cop pulled him over. It seems the cop was the brother of my dad's business partner. He escaped without a ticket. He had absolutely no patience whatsoever for dumb driver and I am exactly the same. My dad used to drive two hours a day in Los Angeles traffic just going to and from work, so I guess that had something to do with his driving habits. So, when I take to the highway, even in my younger, carefree days, I was still an intense driver. This is where the story begins.

Tommy and I decided to leave Sonoma valley and head north. We stopped in and filled up the gas tank, got our groceries and beers for the day and took off about an hour behind schedule. I get very impatient when I fall behind in a driving schedule. Tommy was carefree and never let anything bother him, so he was a nice vacation partner. I'm behind the wheel of my old blue and V.W. van as we enter the freeway. All is fine until a half an hour later, when Tommy gets this funny look on his face. I ask him what is wrong and he says he has to take a dump. I get furious. Is that ridiculous? I get mad when he has to take a dump. We were falling behind in our schedule, we had just been to the store that had a bathroom, and now, he had to take a dump. I feel bad about it now, but I refused to pull over for him. I was on the freeway, had the old van up to sixty m.p.h. and we were on a roll. It took quite a bit of coaxing to get that van up to sixty miles an hour. He begged and pleaded with me, told me he would never do it again, but I still refused. What a weenie I was. I recently spoke to Tommy and he had forgotten about this adventure, so I didn't feel too bad. He didn't take it too bad, he sat there for awhile reading the newspaper until he started squirming. He got up from his seat and crouched his way into the rear of the van. I was busy driving, so I didn't pay much attention, but he asked me if we were doing anything with an empty coffee can. I couldn't believe my eyes. I look back and there he is holding this empty Folgers's coffee can. I then knew what he had in mind and I was in awe. I knew then, I was in the company of greatness. He had this big grin on his face as he slid his pants down to his ankles. Mind you, I'm driving sixty miles an hour on the freeway and there is Tommy, squatting, trying to hit a coffee can with his dump. He had balls, and on that day, they were huge. He had only two arms, so he had to decide how to use them. Would he use one to hold the can to his butt and the other to brace himself, or would he hold the can

with both hands and trust me to drive smoothly. Neither, he was so sure of

himself and his aim, he used both hands to hold onto the back of his seat, while

his sphincter took aim at the can. I was in amazement and this was one of the

greatest feats ever witnessed. I tried to hold the van steady, but I remember a

slight cross wind and if you have ever driven a van, you know they swerve when a

gust of wind hits. Tommy was calm, cool and collected. I broke down and

offered to pull over, but he was determined at that point to finish the job. I had to

drive, but I also wanted to watch this amazing event happening in my van.

I kept one eye on the road and the other on Tommy. He squatted and even

chatted with me as we cruised down the highway. The wind hit us a few times,

causing the van to swerve, but Tommy had nerves of steel. I was imagining a turd

landing on the carpet, but he kept his cool and compensated for the curve. He was

playing the shift, like an America's cup skipper. The I looked back to see the first

and biggest turd emerge and graze the side of the coffee can, but skip into the

middle of the container. What an event! I was losing my focus. I was more

interested in watching him dump, than I was in driving down the freeway. The

smell hit me like a blast of hot air from a furnace. The smell was bad, but we had

partied pretty hard the night before, so I cut him some slack. I couldn't expect him to take a sweet smelling dump in a coffee can while driving down the freeway could I? He did overlook one very important element, the toilet paper; it was in the far back of the van in our luggage. Our options were limited at that point. I could pull over, Tommy could duck walk with his pants at his ankles to try to make into a bathroom, or we could find an alternative wiping source. We opted for number two, because I found some fast food napkins stuffed in the front seat. Tommy finished the dirty deed, and he knew he had a become a legend in the dumping annals of time. I then managed to pull over to the side of the highway to let him pour out his "coffee grounds". I don't think he wanted to, but I made him. He would have saved them and had them bronzed if I let him. Whenever we spoke of this happening, we spoke in revered tones, both of us respecting the sanctity of this momentous event.

Blowing my knee out

I briefly precluded this upcoming story earlier in the book. I blew my out while taking a dump. I didn't just sprain it, or twist it, I blew it out to the point of having to go to the doctor and get it drained with a needle. If you ever have the option of getting your knee drained or taking pills to get rid of the swelling, go for the pills, trust me. To set the scene, I must backup a bit. This story telling style is

an inherited trait, all of us Gray's take twenty minutes to tell a five minute story.
In January of 1999, I had to go in for surgery on my right Achilles. I had been
having pain in it for three months, so my Podiatrist suggested surgery. The
surgery went fine and I came home the same day. I was prescribed some
Percodan for my heel, when it acted up, and as I have mentioned earlier, I don't
fool around with pain; I take the pills every four hours as directed. I took off
about three weeks and I laid around in bed watching TV. I figured out the daily
television schedule and I had it down to a science. I knew what time certain
shows were on and what channels they came on. I knew from the day before what
would be happening on the show today. I was caught in zombie television land. I
watched Beverly Hills 90210 for the first time and I got hooked. I watched E.R.
for the first time and got hooked. I even got into Chicago Hope for the first time.
So, here I was all hopped up on goof balls, watching reruns of these shows and
crying whenever a semi sad or happy scene came on. I felt like a real jerk off, but
I stuck right to my pain pill prescription.

Everything was going fine until the fourth day rolled around and I realized that
I hadn't taken a bowel movement since my surgery. Panic hit me and I was in
shock, much like Dylan in 90210 when he found out his dad had been murdered!
All I was doing was lying around crying, when I knew deep down that I should

not have been concentrating on dumping. I had this huge cast on my right leg, so it was hard getting around. It came up past my knee, which made maneuvering very difficult. For the first few days I kept myself pretty doped up, only getting up to pee. I had started using the crutches, but I was so screwed up, I nearly fell every time I got up. I crawled to the bathroom until I got used to walking on the crutches while under the influence of Percodan. Like I mentioned, day four was a revelation for me. I cut down on the pain pills in hopes of working up a dump. The next day rolled around after a sound sleep and I felt the mouse. I was overjoyed, the mouse was back. Elaine was pulling huge hours at work while I was down, so I had the house to myself most of the time, but I had nobody to share this great news with. I worked the mouse for only a few minutes, I knew how a bowel movement worked when on pain pills; you took it when it came and didn't fool around. I followed my own advice and crutched my way into the bathroom. I used one arm on the toilet seat and the other on a towel rack on the other wall to lower myself onto the toilet. I soon realized how tough this exercise was going to be. The huge cast on my right leg did not allow me to sit on the toilet with my usual stance. I had to completely straighten out my right leg because the cast wouldn't allow me to bend my leg. I'm now sitting on the pot with my right leg outstretched, bumping into the bathroom wall, trying to find a comfortable position for my left leg. I looked like one of those ballerinas standing with one leg up on the bar while stretching. I was miserable. I couldn't get comfortable, my right leg was pounding and the mouse was starting to retreat. I managed to get my left leg bent a little in hopes of getting some cheek separation for the wipe. The pooplet dump came and went without fanfare. I was discouraged, pissed off and my heal was pounding even harder. I managed a half assed wipe, like I needed one, and flushed the toilet. At least I had the monkey off my back, I did take a dump, and I had that going for me. This was the first dump for me after a major surgery, so I was new to the nuances of how to get up from a toilet with a huge cast on my leg. To back up a little bit, I need to tell you that I have had two major surgeries to my left knee when I was a teenager, so my left knee isn't exactly a pillar of strength. I sat on the toilet and tried a few times to get up without hurting my Achilles or tearing a towel rack off the wall. Neither method worked. I should have just said "screw it", and crawled back to bed, but nooooo, I had to get fancy. I finally decided to be a man and pull myself up with my right arm on the bathroom sink vanity with the majority of power coming from my left knee. I braced myself for the worst and started pulling myself up to the comfort of my crutches. I didn't think too much about the "pop" I heard come from my left knee, and in fact, it didn't even hurt too much. I thought it was my old knee telling me to take it easy. I made my way into bed and promptly popped a few more Percodan's. I deserved a reward, I had just taken a bowel movement.

I woke up a few hours later to some pain coming from left knee and I couldn't believe my eyes when I pulled the bed sheets down. It was swelled up like a baseball. I hung out in bed all day not knowing what to do. Here I was with my right leg in a cast, sitting atop four pillows surrounding with ice packs, and a left knee that seemed to be swelling in front of my eyes. I called my doctor and asked him if the surgery could have done something to my left knee. (I must have sounded like a rocket scientist with that question). He suggested ice on my knee, which is what every doctor recommends. He thought it could be a gout attack. I have had gout for over twenty years and I knew I was in trouble if that was the case. I was a real piece of work when Elaine came home from work that evening. I had ice on my right heal, ice on my left knee, both legs up on pillows as high as I could place them and me, freaked out on Percodan. She tried to settle me down and said, " What the hell happened to you?". I had time to think it over, so I was prepared to tell her that I thought I blew my knee out while taking a dump. She walked over to my medicine table looked at the emptiness of the bottle, shook her head and walked out of the room. I think I heard her say, "Unbelievable".

I watched my knee balloon up for two more days before I decided to go see another doctor. I kid you not, my knee was the size of a softball, if not bigger. Elaine went to the doctor's office with me while he examined my knee. This had to be one of my most embarrassing moments. He looked at the cast on my right leg and looked me in the eye. He then said, " You obviously haven't been doing a lot of physical activity recently, how did you do this?". I sheepishly looked at Elaine and she shakes her head and looks down to the floor. I then look at the doctor and said, " I think I blew my knee out while taking a dump". I will admit, he was a professional about the whole thing, but I bet after I hobbled out of that office, they had a damn good laugh at my expense.

The Supermarket

This is a coming of age story about yours truly. I have mentioned before in this book that I have been enchanted with bowel movements for a long time. I can't exactly pinpoint when I became obsessed with them, but this story might be the beginning.

I spent my college years in San Diego, attending San Diego State University. Those were some of the best days of my life. I worked my way through college working at various restaurants, until I finally earned my degree in Journalism. I sure did a lot with that degree. Here I am selling real estate in Washington state, writing a big book about bowel movements. I'm sure my client data base will love a copy of this bestseller. Anyway, I took out a student loan, bought a Nikon camera and a sailboat to live on. It was an easy, simple and carefree existence. I lived on my first boat for a few years until I upgraded to a thirty foot sloop. This story takes place in a supermarket, while shopping for a two day sailing adventure.

I quit wearing underpants in high school. I can remember the exact day and time I decided to quit wearing undies. I was a catcher on the varsity baseball team and I was squatted down, warming up my best friend and pitcher, Mike McCarthy. Mike had great control, not much of a curve ball, but great control. I always wore a cup when catching because I cherished my testicles, but with Mike I knew I didn't need one, he never put the ball in the dirt. We were warming up when he put one in the dirt, right in front of me. I should have scooped it up, but I missed. The ball bounced and hit me right in the testicle zone. Coach Hilke came over, picked me up off the ground and dropped me back down to the turf. He did this several times until I felt better. What I didn't realize, was that he was trying to drop my testicles to drop out of my abdomen and back down to normal.

From that day on, I decided that I always wanted my testicles down there where they belonged and that underwear would just hinder their freedom.

Now that I have given you a brief history of my underwear feelings, I can proceed. Cary Greer and I decided to take my sailboat out to the Coronado islands for a few days of partying and surfing. Cary and I have known each other since fourth grade, in Mission Viejo, California. I think it was spring break and he was in town for a week or so, taking a break from his studies at U.C.S.B. He was also good friends and former roommate of Tommy, from the previous story. As you have probably noticed, my friends and I gravitated toward the funner colleges. I can't see a Harvard graduate writing a book on bowel movements, unless it had some twist on how it effects the massive globalization of the world or something. I remember the day we decided to go sailing. We sat down and put together a list for a few days at sea. Beer was at the top of the list of course, but we needed some food. We finished making up the list, hopped in my V.W. van and drove to the supermarket. It was a beautiful sunny day with a slight northwest breeze, perfect for our expedition the next day. Cary and I were very good friends and we spoke of bowel movements, but it wasn't a major topic of our conversations. Cary was about to witness the hilarity of Kelly P. Gray losing control of the mouse, in a public place.

I distinctly remember standing in the produce aisle when I felt a dump come on like a tidal wave. It was one of those that you feel come from your lower chest, with your stomach gurgling the whole time. I felt this dump shoot it's way all the way down my stomach and into my abdomen. I barely got the words out, " Cary, I got to take a dump", when it shot out my butt hole, into my shorts and down my leg. There was no stopping at go, no go directly to jail, this dump went straight from my bowels down my leg. It had about the same speed as lava being ejected in a volcanic eruption, and it felt as hot. Now you know why I included the underpants story, you see, I wasn't wearing any. I'm a shorts guy, I love to wear shorts and I don't care how cold it is. I bring a pair of shorts with me on many days when I go into my office, just so I can change into them, the minute I get into my car to leave. I hate long pants and I hate ties. I'd like to meet the jerk off who invented the suit and tie sometime in a dark and deserted alley. I like my shorts comfy, a little big with stretchy waists and huge legs. I can't stand to be fettered in a pair of pants, so what I'm getting at here, is that I was wearing a pair of pants you could drive a Mack truck through. A pair of steel belted Depends wouldn't have stopped this dump. Cary and I spent the previous evening indulging in beer and booze, so it was no surprise that this dump came on with so much fury. I can still picture Cary's face when he looked down and saw runny,

Hot shit running down my leg in the produce section of a Safeway. I think he was in shock. I moved quickly to control the situation, I immediately found a paper towel and gave myself a good wipe up and down the inside of my legs. I still got some on my hand however. Cary's shock had now turned into pure hysterical laughter. He was not helping the situation. I never thought supermarket's had bathrooms, so I knew I had to escape some how unnoticed. I now know different, because I now use our local Safeway's bathroom on a semi regular basis. I immediately scurried my way down the aisle and toward the exit, but not without drawing attention to myself. The manager probably thought I was shoplifting, but I knew he wouldn't want to check my shorts for stolen goods. Cary was following trying to conceal his laughter. I saw a small restaurant across the parking lot, I made a dash for it. I had stopped the flow temporarily, but I knew it wouldn't last, the dike would blow again. The parking lot was huge, it seemed as vast as the Sahara desert. I told Cary to get the car and pick me up, I didn't want to sit in my car with poop running all over the place. I quickly entered the front door of the restaurant with my cheeks clenched, smelling like a Porta Pottie, and asked if I could use their bathroom. That was my huge mistake, you never ask an establishment if you can use their bathroom because ninety percent of the time they will say no. I've never understood that mentality. The odds were right, they turned me down! Just fifteen minutes earlier, I was a happy go lucky, slightly hung-over college student without a care in the world, and now, I was standing in the lobby of some run down, family restaurant with shit running down my leg, smelling like a septic tank.

I had only one course of action left, I had to go outside and rid myself of this foul mess once and for all. I was prepared to take off my shorts and pour dirt on myself and my shorts to rid myself of this monster poop. I saw Cary driving across the lot to meet me, but I must have looked like I had just robbed the place, because he told me I had this wild man look on my face, looking right then left, and finally I took off around to the back of the restaurant. The gods must have been smiling on me that day, because I found a hose in the restaurant's trash area. I didn't just hose off my leg because my shorts were still full of greasy, hot poop. I took off my shorts, stood there naked to the world, and proceeded to wash out my shorts, my crotch and my legs with their hose. To this day, when I see Cary, he will look at me with a funny look on his face and say, " Kelly, I got to take a dump".

Twas the night before Christmas

Bob Howse is a good friend of mine and he definitely loves a good bowel movement story, so it comes as no surprise that he is the main character in a few of the upcoming stories. We confer on an almost daily basis regarding our bowel movements and I must admit, he can hold his own with the best of them. Bob has a different style than I, he uses the multi - dump method. He takes more dumps than anyone I know, and according to him, they are all of good volume. We all know that you can take fifteen dumps a day, but the quality has to drop off somewhere. You probably know someone who is constantly bragging about how many dumps they take a day, but you and I know they are full of shit. Bob still claims that he can take three to five dumps a day and still produce a legal sized dump. A legal dump is one that can be weighed on a scale, smelled from afar and requires proof of soiled toilet paper. I don't spend enough time with him to evaluate his every dump, but assures me it is the truth. This is a Christmas story brought to you by none other than Robert Howse. This story might even replace the fabled, "Night before Christmas", as the new Christmas classic.

Bob works the morning shift from 5:30 am. to 2:30 p.m. and he loves that shift. He likes getting up in the morning, going to work and getting home in time to still do things. I believe it was the Christmas of 1998 that this story takes place. Bob's parents lived about three hours south of our area, and they wanted Bob to get off work on Christmas Eve and drive down for the weekend. Bob was not liking this idea at all. His mother had a nasty habit of ragging on him constantly about everything, you know, like most moms. The idea of having to work all day, then get on the freeway on Christmas Eve and drive three hours wasn't making him a happy guy. He preferred to come over to our house for our traditional prime rib dinner and cocktails, go home early and come back over for Christmas day with all the festivities. Bob was hating the fact of having to make this trek, but he is a good son and he obliged, but there were storm clouds on the horizon for young Bob Howe.

The drive home from Bob's work to his home is only a twenty minute drive without traffic, but when Boeing lets out, the entire town turns to gridlock. His ordinary twenty minute drive can sometimes turn into a gnarly forty five minute, intense drive. This was to be the case on December 24th, 1998. Bob waited by the time clock to get a jump on his exit. He had not used the " Six P's", in his planning. You know, *prior planning prevents piss poor performance*, so he had to drive northward toward home to get his things, then turn around and head south for the drive. This lack of strategy would bury him. Bob got a good jump on the traffic, out of the parking lot, but this is when he first felt the pang of the mouse, the call of the wild, and the train coming into the station. He got into his jeep and hurried down the freeway, thinking he could out race the formidable dump that was brewing inside him. He was wrong. In his own words, he says, " I was sucking my seat cushions up my ass because I was clenching my ass so hard." He told me that he felt it let up as he crossed the trestle toward home, but this mouse was playing for keeps. The traffic was bad, but he had seen worse, so he remained optimistic. The reprieve from the mouse was only a ruse, the mouse had no intention of letting up, he was going for the kill. Bob crossed over the Snohomish river, he suddenly felt the poop make a sudden jump toward his pants. He squeezed even harder, but the mouse was relentless. He got closer to his home without incident, he was holding his own. He even had a chance to pull over to a nearby gas station before he got home, but his will and sheer desire took him all the way home in hopes of making it to his beloved toilet. All he could think of was his toilet, his comfortable surroundings, his sanctuary. Bob actually made it to his driveway without shitting his pants, he thought he beat the odds. I think he made a huge mistake next; he made a mad dash for his front door. As we have read before in this book, the mad dash does not increase your odds for beating the nasty diarrhea dump. He should stopped, taken his time, pinched his cheeks a little harder and walked very carefully into his happy little home.

Bob raced out of his Jeep and made it to the front door. He fumbled with his keys and as he did, he felt a huge amount of poop come shooting out of his butt. " It was pudding poop", says Bob. As he unlocked his front door, he unbuckled his belt and all hell broke loose. He said there was poop everywhere. As he raced toward the bathroom, it came gushing out into his under pants, overflowed those and started running down his legs. By the time he reached the bathroom, there was very little left in his system. He dropped his pants to the floor and poop came spewing out all over the place. It overflowed from his undies into the bathroom floor, onto his socks and completely covered the toilet. The pudding poop was in his undies, on his legs, in his pants, on his socks, and last but not least, all over his new carpet. Bob says his undies looked like someone had poured a newly mixed batch of concrete into them. There were no survivors. He had to throw away his undies and his socks. He sat and looked at the destruction and could not believe the volume of poop sitting in his pants. He sat there in disbelief, trying to fathom what had just happened to him. He got himself together, stepped into the shower along with his pants and proceeded to wash down. He had been beaten and he knew it. Bob got cocky, he gambled and lost. I wonder how Santa handles it when he has a case of diarrhea on Christmas Eve? Bob had to get on his hands and knees to scrub all the pudding poop out of his new carpet. He said he could see the trail of poop from the front door to the bathroom. Whenever he tells the story, he always emphasizes the amount of poop and how fast it came rushing out of his butt. And just think, this was just the start of his Christmas weekend with his parents. Merry Christmas to all and to all a good dump!

The Dream Dump

This story is not going where you think it's going, it is another sad story involving our friend Bob. Bob is a very eligible bachelor and maybe his bowel habits have something to do with that, but he takes his movements seriously, but can also laugh at his own follies. Bob recently had a dump story experience in bed. You'd think with a dump history like mine and Bob's, that we'd be going to one of the encounter meetings for help. I can see Bob standing up at one of these meetings and saying, " I'm Bob and I'm a dumpaholic." I may be laughing, but I'll be sitting right next to him. This is a very innocent story with a not so happy ending.

Bob, like I mentioned, lives on his own, thank God! He recently revealed a dump story to me that merited a mention in this good humored romp through the wacky world of bowel movements. It seems that Bob was having a pleasant night's sleep when his dreams took over. We have all had those dreams that when you get up, we think they were real, well, Bob's was. Bob was fast asleep in his comfy, cozy bed when his dreams turned nasty. I don't mean nasty in the naked girl sense, but in the ugly, terrible sense. You see, Bob dreamed that he took a dump in his bed, and alas, some dreams do come true.

Bob tells it like this. He's asleep in his bed when he dreams that poop was running down his butt cheeks. He can't recall whether he is awake or asleep at this point, but he farts a solid mass. I don't think I would admit to being awake on this one. So he dreams that he is taking a dump, then farts. That seems harmless enough, unless he actually does it, which he did. I've wet my bed and thrown up in my bed, but never pooped it. I remember wetting the bed when I was a kid and I would do everything imaginable to hide it from my parents. I even turned my mattress over a few times, hoping they wouldn't find the evidence. Now imagine if Bob turned over his mattress after shitting in it! Bob pooped in his bed and woke up to the horror. I wish I could change the scenario a bit to spice up the story. What if Bob had been in bed with someone? Maybe he was, and just won't admit it. What a turn off to wake up next to someone in a pile of shit. I remember a Playboy Playmate of the month saying in her turn ons and turn offs question, that she hated waking up with a guy in a pile of shit.

He woke up in a cold sweat. He smelled something and then reverted back to his dream. He thought, whew, what a stinky fart, but to his horror , he felt something hot, mushy, stinky and runny between him and his sheets. He remembers saying out loud to himself, " I just shit myself!" I think back to the scene from "The Godfather", when the Hollywood director wakes up next to the severed head of his favorite horse, lying next to him in his bed. This is a judgment call, but I think I could handle the horse's head better than a pile of fresh, steaming crap.

Bob looked down and saw that his dream wasn't a dream after all. He had, indeed taken a dump in his bed. What a great place to take a dump. I can't imagine a more comfortable place to take a dump. We all try to make our little toilets a very homey and comfortable place to take a dump, but it could never match the comfort level of your bed. In a weird and perverted way, I kind of envy Bob for pulling this off. As long as I live, I will probably never feel the comfort of dumping while in the prone position. My dad, Larry, loved the prone position. In fact, we think he passed away while watching a football game in the lying down position. Don't think I'm morbid here, if I had my choice of how I'd like to pass away, I think my dad's way doesn't look too bad. My old man used to think that there ought to be couches or beds at professional baseball games, so you could get really comfortable. He was a strange guy, but I loved him.

Back to Bob's dilemma, how did he handle waking up to a bed full of poop? He was shocked and dismayed at what lay before him. He could swear that he just dreamed taking a dump, he never imagined waking up with one in his bed. He handled matters like a true professional. After he declared that he had "just shit himself", Bob cupped his ass with both of his hands and carefully walked into the bathroom. He not only had poop running all over himself and in his hands, but he still had to go! After sitting on the pot for a few anxious minutes, Bob took the Kelly way out, and jumped in the shower to make sure he got a good cleaning. Once out of the shower, he still had to remove the poop laden sheets from his bed and carefully carry them into the laundry room, where he promptly started a load. He ended up throwing away his undies and his socks. When he heard the gentle sound of his washing machine in it's rinse cycle, he crawled onto his living room couch and quickly fell asleep. He woke up rested, showered with a clean set of sheets ready for the dryer. Not a bad night's work if you ask me.

The Gold Crown

I am the youngest of three boys. My oldest brother Gary is nine years older than me and my second older brother Mike is six years my senior. We grew up in a middle class family and we had a great childhood. Pat and Larry did a great job raising us, but we all wanted to go to college and that wasn't in the budget. Gary graduated from U.C.L.A., Mike from U.C.S.B. and myself from San Diego State. Our folks helped us when they could, but for the most part, we all worked our way through college. Mike was the brain and the athlete, so he had scholarship money for a few years. Gary did his best working odd jobs and selling his sperm on occasion. I, on the other hand worked my way through college by working in the restaurant business. What a blast, but that is the subject for my next novel. We had a cousin named William, who we spent every summer together with at Newport Beach. Pat and Larry would go in on a beach house with our Uncle Will and Aunt Marge, every year. William was a cool cousin, but instead of spending all his spare time at the beach like we did after high school, he decided to go to Dental School. He graduated from U.S.C. and had his license hanging in his own office within three years. There is a point to this story, I promise! I used to call him up once in awhile when I was living on my own in college, with a tooth and he would council me on what to do, or have me drive up to L.A. to have him work on it. I was bartending and waiting tables at the Chart House in San Diego, so I was always munching on something. Ah, the days of being able to eat as much as you wanted and never gain a pound. Anyway, I was chewing on something, when I felt something fall out of my mouth. I emptied the contents of my mouth into my hand and there lie a gold crown. It had been in my mouth for a long time, I think I had it put in when I was a kid. I freaked out because I had this huge hole in my mouth and the cold air was making it hurt like a son of a bitch. I tried to put it back in my mouth and make it fit on the tooth, but I slipped and I ended up swallowing it! I swallowed my gold crown!

On my way home, I stopped off and got a piece of gum to put over my exposed tooth for the night. I was definitely freaked out, and it hurt too. I immediately called Skip the next morning and asked him what to do. He suggested going to a local dentist to have him put in a temporary crown until I could make it up to see him. As most college students are, I was very money conscious and I asked him how much all this was going to cost. He told me the temporary shouldn't be too much, but that a new gold crown was going to cost about five hundred dollars. Five hundred dollars! It might as well have been five million dollars to a college student. I told him there was no way I could afford that. He thought a moment and then came up with a brilliant plan. He said that if I could recover my crown and bring it up to him, that he could get it done for practically free! What a great idea, I loved it, until I thought about it. I wasn't going to have my stomach pumped, so the only other way that I knew of retrieving something I ate was to either throw it up, and it was too late for that, or look for it in my poop. Yep, that was the plan.

You have to keep in mind that five hundred dollars was a lot of money to me back in 1982. Desperate times require desperate measures. I asked him how long it would take for my crown to pass through my system and he said, "Oh, it shouldn't take more than a day or two." This relieved me somewhat, because I was on a one dump a day routine back then, so what if I had to finger my way through one or two of my dumps, I could handle it. Now there were a few things I didn't think about right away, like how would I go through my bowel movement and where I would let out the load. I lived on my sailboat at the time in Mission Bay, so I was usually taking my dumps in the public toilet every morning. My first thought was, how was I going to take a dump in the toilet and then start to look through it in a public bathroom. Can you imagine walking in on someone sifting through a pile of hot steaming crap ? My second thought was, what was I going to use to look through my poop? A magnifying glass? I only had a few hours to figure it out, so I had to think fast. The mouse was beginning the descent. I opted for the most private method.

My plan was to lay newspaper down on the carpeted floor of my boat. I would squat over the paper, take the dump and proceed to go through it with a fork. So I was killing two birds with one stone, I was taking a dump on day old newspaper that had to be thrown away anyway, so why not throw it away with poop wrapped inside of it. I was quite the recycler. I went to the grocery store early that morning and bought myself a pair of those heavy duty, rubber dish washing gloves. I still remember, they were bright yellow. I got back from the store and I felt the first bowel movement coming on, so I had to gather everything as fast as I could. I put on my gloves, laid out the newspaper and got my trusty fork ready for action. At first I was optimistic, you see, I mistook every peanut for my gold crown. I had eaten trail mix the night before when I swallowed my crown. If you don't know how much a gold crown looks like a cashew or a peanut, you do now. So there I was, pooping in the middle of my boat with a fork in one hand while my other hand held me steady. After I pooped and wiped, (I put the toilet paper in the toilet), I then got down on my hands and knees with my trusty fork and proceed to sift through my raunchy smelling dump. If this wasn't the lowest part of my life, what was? The first dump was a nightmare. I had to get within inches of my fresh dump to examine it for the tooth. My nose would have ended up in the middle of the pile if there was a slight rocking of the boat. It was sickening, disgraceful and downright demeaning. My first bowel movement was not a success. Taking the dump wasn't so bad, in fact it reminded me of squatting and dumping in the woods. I must have spent a half an hour on that first dump. The peanuts threw me for a loop. I must have thought ten times that I had found it, but after bringing the nuggets closer to my eyes, I noticed that they were indeed peanuts or cashews. I took the fork and smooshed it down into the poop and then smear it around, in hopes of finding a solid, shiny object lying there. Another demeaning feature to this little exercise of the damned, was that I was worried that I may somehow pick the crown in my toilet paper while wiping and flush it down the toilet. After wiping myself, I flushed the paper into my bilge system. I even had to run the toilet paper around my anus to make sure the crown hadn't stuck to my butt cheeks. I opened up the hatch of the boat and sat out on the deck for awhile. I was worried I didn't lay enough paper down, I didn't want any seepage.

Believe it or not, my farts also worried me. What if I was sitting in one of my women's studies courses, and I let loose a really gnarly fart? What would I do? Raise my hand and ask the professor if I could drop my drawers to see if there was a gold crown in my pants? I actually thought a lot about the fart factor.

You'd think that I would feel a sharp object shoot out my anus and hit my leg, but wasn't sure. This was definitely a low point for me; I actually considered wearing underpants for the first time since high school. My carefree days were over. I was constantly thinking about the stupid gold crown lost somewhere in my colon. The first day passed, then the second and the third rolled around. I had never been so aware of what I was putting into my body as I was then. I wouldn't eat anything that resembled a crown, so that ruled out most roughage, which contributed to the quality decline of my bowel movements. I stuck to yogurt, soups and toast for the first few days, and then I became less enthusiastic. Will told me a few days, but I still hadn't found it after four days and nine dumps. I was still getting up every morning, spreading out the newspaper, then spreading out my cheeks and dumping on the floor of my boat. I have never quite looked at a fork the same way again after this incident. You constantly read about these new diets coming out all the time; low Carb, high fiber, high protein, all pizza, whatever. I came up with the best diet ever, just spread out a newspaper every morning and take a dump on it, then sift through your bowel movement with a fork. This would be the best diet on the market. You see, after you have looked at your poop, up close and sitting on a fork, you really take time to consider what you've been eating. I did, and I came away from this experience a better man and a little more considerate of my digestive system.

To make a very long and miserable story short, I will let you know that I was still searching for that little five hundred dollar gem after a week. The process didn't even bother me after day five. It had become a ritual, I had been reduced to an animal. The only difference between myself and one of my dogs is that I used a fork. I think my neighbors on the dock started becoming a little suspicious after a few days when I would come walking up the dock every day with a small bundle of wrapped up newspaper. They must have thought I was doing some sort of wicked experiment on rodents or something. I did tell my friends about my dilemma, I wasn't proud. They will probably never forget it. How many people have you met in your life, that had to sift through their poop every morning with a fork? It reminds me of yet another story of my youth, when I swallowed three cupcake wrappers and my mom had to look through my poop to make sure they wouldn't get caught in my intestines. Poor Pat. My buddies asked me everyday how the search was coming, and I even developed a mini cult following from my regulars at the bar where I bartended. Some people would come in to have a drink, just to hear about my poop searching progress. I don't think my manager much appreciated it, but what the hell. I was bringing in business and making pretty good tips. I don't know how I decided to quit searching my bowel

movements, what is the difference between seven days and eleven? A lot!,
believe me. I quit sifting after seven days. I had enough humiliation and decided
to walk away. The five hundred dollars seemed trivial at that point and I couldn't
go on any longer. I never found the crown, but I learned some very important
things about life. First, I saw up close and personal what my bowel movements
looks like for an entire week, and I must say there were some stellar dumps.
Second, I learned a great lesson in humility and shared some pretty raucous
laughs with friends, at my expense. Third, I realized that five hundred dollars
wasn't really worth that much. Fourth, and the most important lesson I learned
from that experience, is that people really care about bowel movements and that if
you share your bowel movement follies with those you love, you will all become
a little bit closer.

Gary

I have mentioned my oldest brother Gary a few times throughout this book.
He was the first person to teach me some life lessons and I am appreciative. I feel
I owe him some print space in this book because he deserves it, he brings another
dimension to the perverted world of bowel movements. I have to preface these
next few stories with a little background. The men in our family have the un-

fortunate malady called gout. Not to get too technical, but this is a kidney disease in which our kidneys don't break down Purines in foods that turn into acidic crystals that form in joints in your body. Certain foods are very high in purines with the worst being beef and booze. This is why it used to be called the disease of Kings. Now these crystals are extremely painful and not just a pain or throb, but full blown screaming, crawling across the floor pain that is very hard to convey to anyone who hasn't had it. Needless to say, when a gout attack hits, it usually shows up in the big toe, thus rendering us unable to walk for days on end until we get rid of it. I'm getting to my point, I promise. Now, if we took the responsible way to get rid of these Purines, we would put our foot up, drink massive amounts of water and wait 3-7 days until we passed it out of our systems. It is hard to call into work with gout because it has a stigma bout it that if you have gout, you are some type of heathen. Well….. No, I won't go there. Anyway, we opt for medicine called Colchicine which when enough does are taken, you start shitting pure yellow poop that smells rancid and we don't have any control of when we will have to hit the head. That is the bad part of the Colchicine shits, the good part is that when this starts, we know the Gout is coming to an end. Now, on to Gary. I mentioned his skid marks earlier. If there were an Olympic event, he would bring home the gold every four years. A perfect example of this is when my brother Mike, Gary and I were in southern California laying my mom, Pat to rest and we each had our own hotel rooms. Mike and I were up early and knocked on Gary's door to get him up. We were going to play a Memorial round of golf. Gary opened up his door and to our horror, our eyes, Mike's wife Tina included, were fixed on his bed sheets. The three inch wide skid mark looked like a tire mark, running about two feet in length. I think I said, " Should we have your maid change your sheets to toilet paper?" Tina was aghast, "My God", she said and we all looked at each other in disbelief. I don't think I have ever had that much poop on one of my wipes on the toilet. "Gary, did you use your sheets to sleep under or to wipe yourself", Mike said. Gary was completely unfazed and in fact, proud of his accomplishment. " What is the problem, this is nothing". Tina, Mike and I looked at Gary, his sheets and then burst out in laughter. From that day forward, I have held his wife in high esteem for having to put up with this outlandish behavior for so many years.

The Teacher

Gary is an educated man who holds a Master's Degree in Education. He just recently retired from teaching at a very prestigious school in Hawaii. He calls me on occasion to give me details on a recent dumping mishap and we share a good laugh. This last story is one for the ages.

It seems Gary was trying to dress the part of scholar in his last years, probably due to a school mandate, because he would live in shorts 24/7 if he could, just like all the Gray men. He went to school very early in the morning to get his lesson plan in order and to be ready for his students arrival. On this day, Gary wore a light fabric, pair of light khaki pants along with his aloha shirt. As he sat at his desk alone in his classroom and his thoughts, he felt the mouse poking out and the mouse was in a much bigger hurry than Gary thought. Gary underestimated the power of the mouse.

As Gary raised up from his chair, it was already too late, the lava was flowing out his butthole, into his pants and down his legs. You see, he was on the tail end of a Colchicine recovery. Gary and I share another trait, we don't wear underwear. I know what you are thinking and we deal with the consequences on our own terms, but that is beside the point. I will admit though, undies probably would have helped out in this situation. Gary knew he had to think quick, because his pants were covered in shit and his students were about to arrive. He clenched his buns together and slowly ran into the bathroom. Luckily, it was still early enough to not be detected by any fellow teachers.

As he dropped his pants to the floor with poop running out all over the floor, he quickly took a page out of my book and proceeded to do the major cleanup due to the fact that he had a long day ahead of him with no spare clothes in his car or office. He was methodical, first cleaning his cheeks, then moving down to the floor and toilet seat so all he had left were the pants. The pants were going to be his downfall. After taking multiple swipes inside his pants with wet napkins form the sink, he got most of the poop out of his pants, but there was still a brown ring because of his light colored pants and an extremely wet situation. He figured his pants would dry eventually so he could deal with a wet ass for a few hours, but the stain was worrying him. You can't skimp on the water cleanup.

The stain was about the size of a grapefruit, which is pretty good considering the circumstances, so he decided to teach class from his chair rather than standing up with his ass to the class and writing on the blackboard. As the day progressed, he wondered how long it would take the kids to notice that he hadn't got up from his chair. He then had a problem arise that he hadn't planned for, the odor emanating from his pants. For those of you who have attempted to clean up poop from a fabric know the smell I'm talking about here. It is a sour, damp, putrid smell that travels long distances and is impossible to mask. Gary thought he had a plan. He thought he was smarter than the smell. He was wrong, dead wrong. He called for an early break for the students and allowed them to do some work outside. Funny how that worked out... Gary slowly walked down to the men's room and into the exact stall he had been occupying earlier to complete the dirty deed. He saw what he thought was his answer to all his worries, a can of aerosol spray designed to mask the smell of bowel movements, not shit stained pants. Gray pulled his stained pants down to his ankles and proceeded to spray his stain with the Glade Spray. Ahh, to go through the day with your shitty pants smelling like Gardenias and those Gardenias smelled worse as the day progressed.

Gary confidently sauntered back to his classroom thinking he had beat back the beast, but it was not so. He spent the rest of the spraying his poopy pants with Glade because as it dried every time, the smell became more putrid. He was sickened by his own stench and it doesn't get much worse than that. He was sure the kid in the back row could smell him, but wasn't sure. Let's just say the kids never had so many recesses as they did on this fateful day. The day finally ended after he bowed out of a teacher meeting and he drove happily home with his pants wadded up in the back seat and his bare ass cheeks on the car seat. I don't think Gary ever wore a light colored pair of pants to work again.

Conclusion

I want to thank all of you for reading Log On, The Big Book of Bowel Movements. I want to reiterate that all the preceding stories and anecdotes are accurate and true. I have included a few pages for you to jot down some notes about your thoughts or favorite bowel movement stories. Keep this book in your bathroom or on your dining room table and bring it out for parties and pass it around. Maybe it will become the next craze; Bowel Movement Parties. I am also working on another volume so I would appreciate any feedback or tales of your own, and maybe you will make the next volume. You will soon can find me at www.thebigbookofbowelmovements.com.

The bowel movement is a universal thing, like laughter. I had a Journalism professor in college once say that if you want to write a book, find a topic that everyone can relate to. I hope I have accomplished that. Everyone in the world does it, so why don't we share it? I can't name anything else in the world that we all do but don't speak of. Join me in helping take bowel movements out of the closet. We need more laughter and joy in the world. I also want to thank those individuals who let me use their name in writing of this book.

Notes

Notes

Author's Biography

Kelly P. Gray grew up in southern California. He attended San Diego State University and earned a degree in Photojournalism with a minor in Women's Studies. Kelly spent two years working for the University newspaper, The Daily Aztec as a writer and photographer. Kelly then spent over three years freelancing for Surfer magazine. Kelly spent over thirty years in the Restaurant-Bar-Hotel business, throughout California, Hawaii and Washington.

Kelly met Elaine while working for the Maui Marriott, and have been married since 1988. They now reside in Lake Stevens Washington, with their dogs and cat, daughter Amber resides in Texas with her husband and three children. Kelly and Elaine have now been selling real estate successfully for over twenty years.

Kelly credits his odd perspective on life to his parents, brothers and friends. Growing up in southern California during the seventies and eighties had it's advantages.

Reviews

"His perspective is very Seinfeldian in nature, you will laugh out loud at this book". Bob Howe, Good Friend.

" The stories are the dessert at the end of a great meal, you'll want to share it with everyone". Tom McDonald, Good Friend.

"He takes us through the ABC's of a bowel movement. Required reading for all adults and teens alike." Jake Stub, Good Friend.

"Howling out loud funny, a must for any college dorm room." Eamon Gray, Nephew.

" The bowel movement is finally out of the closet, and what better man to do it." Mike Gray, Brother.

"A must for every Christmas list." Elaine Gray, Wife.

"This book will become an American classic, right up there with Mark Twain, a must for any serious reader's collection". Cary Greer, Good friend.

" This is the ultimate handbook to taking a dump, I read it all in one sitting, then went back for more." Amber, Daughter

" A compelling novel, complete with plot twists and turns. Full of romance, intrigue, mystery, sadness and humor." Gary Gray, Brother.

"After reading this book, I want to give Kelly a great big hug." Stranger on the street.

"The feel good book of the year!". Ululani Holmes, Good Friend.

"This book defines a generation." Liam Gray, Nephew.

Made in the USA
San Bernardino, CA
20 November 2014